When God Works...

A story of Crisis Turned into Victory

Amy Rogers

Edited by Melanie Smith

ISBN 979-8-88616-307-0 (paperback)
ISBN 979-8-88616-308-7 (digital)

Christian Faith Publishing
832 Park Avenue
Meadville, PA 16335
www.christianfaithpublishing.com

Printed in the United States of America

I've had people tell me for years to write a book to share my story. I pushed it off and pushed it off. I let the lies of the devil tell me I shouldn't, tell me that I'm not good enough. And the truth is, I'm not good enough, but I serve a God who is! We've all sinned. We all have things we are not proud of. These are tools the devil uses to keep us silent. We all have stories that need to be shared, no matter how big or small. It's my prayer that, through this book, people will see Jesus—that they will see His power and strength, that they will see He carries us when we can't stand on our own.

A few family members will be sharing their perspectives at the end of the book as well. John 14:10 (NIV) says, "The words I say I do not speak on my own authority. Rather, it is the Father, living in me, who is doing the work." May He get the glory forever and ever. Amen.

Chapter 1

My Upbringing

I grew up in Decatur, Alabama, the middle of three children of Connie and Danny Holaway. I have a younger brother and older sister. I always liked being in the middle and being the only person in our family with red hair. We grew up attending church with our parents. I remember my dad would take my sister and me to early service so that my mom could get ready in peace. (That makes so much more sense now that I'm an adult!) I asked Jesus to come into my heart around the age of ten. I was spending the night at my maw-maw and paw-paw Holaway's house with my sister Lanae and my cousin Alison. They started talking about sin and heaven and hell. I remember the exact spot I was sitting on the bed, looking at a fiber optic lamp, when I realized I was a sinner in need of a savior. I knew that hell would be my eternal destination if I didn't act. I got off the bed, knocked on my grandparents' bedroom door. My paw-paw walked out, wearing a little white tank and shorts. I told him that I wanted to know how to be saved. He walked me over to their brown leather tufted sofa. He walked me through what it meant to be saved, made sure I understood, and then asked if I wanted to get saved. My paw-paw and I knelt down on their sofa, and I asked Jesus to come into my heart. I remember calling my mom right afterward to tell her my news! I was baptized a few weeks later.

I was always involved in activities at church. I just loved being there, whether it was vacation Bible school, children's choir, Girls in Action, camps—really anything. I began going on mission trips with our youth group when I got older. Some of my fondest church memories revolve around mission trips. I have always had an interest in geography and travel. I loved being able to see other parts of the US and world and getting to share Jesus at the same time. I enjoyed getting to know others better while on these trips. The sense of unity on every trip was refreshing and encouraging.

I grew up with fairly large families on both sides. We would spend every holiday and lots of Sundays together. My grandparents on both sides did a wonderful job of pointing us to Jesus. My parents did as well. I honestly can't think of any complaints about the majority of my childhood until around middle school. I was picked on in late elementary school for being chubby. The words kids said were extremely hurtful and did make me struggle for a while about my self-image. I constantly viewed myself as the fat girl. I began to doubt my self-worth going into middle school.

Around this same time, alcohol would begin to seep its way into my family. My dad would occasionally drink to help relax from his workday. Over the years, it would end up becoming an addiction. He was no longer coming to church with us. This was not the dad that I grew up with. This wasn't the dad that took us to early service or that coached our softball teams. Alcohol would eventually rob my dad of everything he once loved. This disease would cause my parents to divorce during my senior year of high school. I was more at peace when I didn't have to live with my dad. I didn't have to worry about hearing him stumble down the hallway to his bed. Out of sight became out of mind, but I would never stop praying that my dad would be freed from his addiction.

After high school, I attended the University of North Alabama. This is where I met the man I would marry, Adam Rogers. I had a crush on him the first time I laid eyes on him at the Baptist Campus Ministries (BCM). We even lived in the same apartment complex during our sophomore year of school, but we never dated. We were both very active in the BCM in various ways. We went on several mission trips together as well. We started becoming a little more acquainted during our final year at UNA. I was dating someone at this time, and we were both going on summer missions. He would be going to the state of Washington, and I was going to China. He and

I both knew that this summer apart would show us if we were supposed to get married or break up. I remember so clearly us breaking up over the phone, thousands of miles apart. It was a mutual breakup and the easiest one I've ever had. We just both knew we weren't supposed to be together.

Going to China was extremely impactful for many reasons. It was my first major solo flight, going from Michigan to Japan alone. I look back on it now and see the amount of faith my parents had to send their daughter across the world alone. Our main focus was witnessing in the pink-light district where places that looked like hair salons were fronts for prostitution. It was heartbreaking to meet women who were selling their bodies. Several did give their hearts to Christ while we were there. Our Chinese interpreters were so excited and willing to share their faith. We also worked with college students on conversational English, using a children's Bible to teach them stories. In China, if you lead someone to the Lord, you get to baptize them. Two students became believers, and one of our summer missionaries had the privilege of baptizing one of the young ladies in the South China Sea. This was a bold step of faith for the new Chinese believers, especially since they could be persecuted for their newfound belief in Christ. Visiting China helped me realize I should never take my freedom of religion for granted!

Upon returning from China, Adam called me out of the blue. Each missionary had made prayer bracelets in different colors to give to prayer partners while we were gone. I had given Adam one of my yellow bracelets and asked him to pray for me while I was gone. He was just calling to see how my summer went, and I was so unexplainably giddy. I had just gotten out of a relationship; I should not be jumping into another one yet! He and I began talking a little more. Something just felt right. Within a month, I knew I was supposed to marry him. I've always heard people say, "When you know, you know!" I finally understood that! There was no doubt in my mind that I was supposed to be his wife. (There is a funny backstory: we were on a creative ministries team at UNA, and we were performing at his home church. I was sick the night before. His dad was the music minister and quite the hugger. I told him that I had been sick, and he probably didn't want to hug me. He said, "Aww, it'll be fine." So I got a sweet hug from him, and then I said, "You know what, if Adam ends up as cute as you, I may just have to marry him." And who knew that I would end up marrying him a year later!) Adam and I were together around six months before he asked me to marry him on February 1, 2005. We had a beautiful wedding on September 17, 2005.

Life was good for us newlyweds until our house was broken into shortly after Christmas. We lost a few items purchased for Christmas, but the most devastating loss was our camera. We no longer had any pictures from our first Thanksgiving or Christmas together. They had broken into our house at a specific time that they knew we wouldn't be home. Adam was working in banking at the time, and I was a children's caseworker at a mental health center. I was beginning to feel like that wasn't what I was supposed to be doing with my life. I didn't feel like that was my true calling. Adam and I prayed about a career change. I truly felt like I was supposed to be a teacher. Little did we know that this decision would change our lives forever.

Chapter 2

The Carjacking

I quit my job at the mental health center and decided to go back to school to work on my master's degree in education. We began living off one income and paying for school. I got accepted into the University of Montevallo's education program. This school was almost two hours away from my house. To save on gas money, I would stay at my sister's apartment in Birmingham a few days a week. I started at Montevallo in the summer of 2006. I was excelling my classes, learning a lot and making new friends. I knew this was exactly what I was supposed to be doing!

On Monday, July 31, I had gotten out of class in the early afternoon. I pulled up to my sister's apartment at around four-thirty. I was sitting in the front seat, starting to gather up the stuff I had placed in my passenger seat. I had my keys in my hand and one foot out of the door when a man approached me with a gun and told me to get back into the car. What was happening?

This is broad daylight. This can't be happening to me. This is the stuff you see happening to people on TV, not to me! As I was getting back into the car, I accidentally leaned on the horn when I was crawling over into the passenger side. I can see the window to Lanae's apartment about ten feet in front of me. Surely, she will see me and get help. Nothing. (Come to find out later that she did look outside the window but never saw me.) The guy asked me for my keys, my phone, and any money I had. Poor guy—he had no clue he was trying to rob someone that's broke as a joke. I gave him my phone and my keys. He also asked me for my credit cards. I told him that I didn't have any. He said, "Come on, all white folks have credit cards."

In my head, I wanted to tell him that we were followers of financial advisor Dave Ramsey, and he didn't believe in credit cards. I kept that bit of information to myself though and told him again that I didn't have any credit cards. I told him I didn't have any money either. I told him that we can go bank hopping to different ATMs for me to get him money. I said, "We can max out every ATM. Just please don't hurt me."

As I was sitting in the passenger seat, my mind was swirling. Adam and I hadn't even been married for a year. What if something happened to me, and I didn't make it? He would be a widower at the age of twenty-five. I immediately started praying as my head was spinning. My prayer went along these lines: "God, I'm scared. I know that You are with me. Please keep me safe."

After I prayed silently, he began to pull out from the parking spot. He took a right out of the apartment complex onto a fairly busy road. I felt safer on this road because there were businesses lining the street. He then took another right into a residential area. As he turned, he looked back and said, "I gotta see where my girl's at."

There was a car following us. I turned around my left shoulder to get a look at the car, but he told me to face the front and not turn around again.

He was keeping the gun propped on his leg, pointing in my direction. I started thinking about things I've seen on TV that you should do if you were ever abducted. I remember them saying that you should make yourself seem more like a person to your captor. So I start trying to talk to him more about our money plan and more about myself. I wonder now why I didn't lie and tell him that I was pregnant. Would he have been nicer to me then? The more I talked, the less he liked it. He put the gun to my head and said, "Say another word. I dare you."

I was sure he could've heard my heart beating at this point. He took a left turn at another intersection. At this point, we were running parallel with Interstate 65. He asked about where a bank was, and I explained to him that I wasn't from around there but that we need to go to the main roads in order to find any ATMs. He took another left turn into a residential area, but this road would eventually take us to the main road. Surely I can get someone's attention when we are back in a more populated area. He started talking to me again. This time, he mentioned putting me in the trunk. I got it! I knew what to do. If he put me in the trunk, I could kick out the taillights, and someone would see me and call for help! Then he mentioned taking me out to the woods. God stopped my thought processes right then and there. They would find my dead body if I were left in the trunk in the Alabama summer. I knew I had to get out of that car. But how?

I started praying again: "God, show me a safe place to jump out of this car." Stupid me had asked the guy earlier if I could buckle my seat belt. I couldn't stand riding in a car without my seat belt fastened, and now I must figure out how to undo the dumb thing *and* jump out of the car quickly. We were approaching an intersection, and I think he thought we had a stop sign, so he was slowing my car down a bit. I looked in front of me and saw a car coming and looked to the right and saw two people sitting on a porch. *This is it. This is my chance. This is God's sign.* I slowly moved my right hand across my waist to quietly unhook my seat belt. I looked him straight in the eyes, moved my hand to my door handle, and jumped out.

Chapter 3

The Shooting

Everything was a blur. I didn't even remember jumping out of the car. All I knew was I was lying on my back on the ground. And I was in pain, an odd pain that felt like I was burning. Maybe I broke something when I jumped out. I looked down at my white T-shirt and saw a red stain, and I realized I had been shot. In that moment, I said, "God, forgive him for what he did. Please save my life." As soon as those words crossed my lips, I thought, *Did I just say that? Maybe I'm holier than I thought I was. Maybe I have a head injury too.* But I did pray that prayer. Those were the words that showed the power of Christ that lives within us.

I leaned over on my right side and could see the driver in the vehicle that was coming toward us before I had jumped out. He was in a convertible and practically hanging out of his car, trying to see what had happened. I later learned that he thought it was some sort of domestic dispute, resulting in me getting pushed out of the car. He came to my aid as well as two others, a young blond and a guy in a Guns N' Roses shirt. I told the two of them that I saw them standing on the porch, so I knew this would be a safe place for me to jump out. They looked at me and said, "We weren't on the front porch. We were inside the house and heard the gunshot. Then we came out here and found you." I know that God let me see angels that day!

The man from the convertible was calling 911, while the others were trying to get in touch with my family. I remember telling the girl that I was really thirsty and felt like something was on my feet. She looked down and saw that I had jumped right into an ant bed.

She began trying to keep the ants from biting me. They were also just about to bring me something for my thirst when the 911 operator told them I couldn't have anything to drink. Within minutes, police, detectives, and EMTs were there. I remember one detective leaning down to talk to me. He asked for a description of the man that shot me. I told him that he was Black, probably around six feet, heavyset with puffy hair and a flat nose. He also asked me if I had seen a car following us. I said, "Yes, it was a new model charcoal-gray Toyota Camry." Well, I never ever saw the car that was following us. Yet again, God intervened and told me what to say. (Come to find out later that was the exact make and color of the vehicle following us.)

One of my angels got in contact with my sister. She was there within minutes. We were seriously that close to her apartment. She was the only family member to see me before I went into surgery. I remember her leaning down to me, telling me that I was going to be okay and that she loved me. She made the ambulance ride with me, and she also became the one in the family to finally get in touch with Adam about what happened. She had tried to call him more than once, but he didn't answer. She finally got him on the line and said, "Adam, Amy has been carjacked and shot. We are in the ambulance on the way to UAB (University of Alabama at Birmingham) Hospital. She's talking and alert. You need to get to Birmingham as fast as possible."

When they got me into the ambulance, I never lost consciousness throughout the entire trip. They were fiddling with all sorts of things. All I knew was that it was a bumpy ride, it was loud, and I was hurting. I was shot in the back, so I was keeping my knees bent to take pressure off the entry wound. One of the paramedics told me that I would need to put my knees down for a minute in order for them to do something. I was having no part in that. I was keeping my knees bent because the pain wasn't as excruciating that way. I was determined to keep them bent. They eventually had to sit on my knees to get whatever done that was needed, and then I got to prop them back up. I'll never forget the blast of hot, humid air when they opened up the ambulance doors once we got to the emergency room.

They rolled me into the ER, and people started swarming me from all directions. I remember a nurse taking off my wedding rings and me wondering if I would ever see them again. They cut off my shirt and bra to check for an exit wound. The bullet had gone through and through. It went into the middle of my back and came out of the left side of my chest. Then I heard them start to cut my jeans. I tried to sit up, and I said, "No, no, no! You don't have to cut my jeans. There's no blood on them. Just let me take them off!"

They would have no part in that either. They just started snipping away. (I found out later that my precious grandmother searched high and low to replace that pair of jeans. Bless her!) Then a British man by the name of Dr. Richard George approached me on my right side. He explained that he's a trauma surgeon and that he was going to be doing exploratory surgery to see what damage had been done. All I could think about was needing to say something snarky about his accent. The last thing I remember before surgery was asking them to make it stop hurting. Then my world went black.

Chapter 4

Initial Shock

I was taken back to surgery around 5:00 p.m. They had told my family it would take a few hours. It took more than a few hours. Word spread very quickly about my accident. It's not every day that a twenty-five-year-old graduate student gets carjacked and shot. My family said over a hundred people dropped everything and went to the hospital. They cried, and they prayed together. They supported each other. Just their presence there meant something to my family. They didn't have to say a word. It was after eleven-thirty before the doctors came out to speak to my family. They told my family that the surgery had gone well but that I had to have my left kidney and spleen removed. They said the bullet nicked my diaphragm and pancreas, but those could heal with time. The doctors also told them that I would be in the ICU for several days before moving to a step-down room. Little did we know that I would bust out of the ICU after only two and a half days. That was another God-thing.

There is no doubt in my mind that God guided that bullet through my body. The doctors said that if the bullet had entered a fragment more to the right, I would've been paralyzed or killed. And how on earth did the bullet go through my back, out my chest, and completely miss any ribs? The bullet went right between two ribs that didn't allow any ricochet. How did that happen? God allowed that to happen. He knew this would happen to me, even before I was conceived. It was all part of His plan to bring glory to His name. Even as I'm typing this, I wonder, *Why me? Why did He allow me to survive when others haven't? Why am I walking when others can't?* This didn't take God by surprise. He can take a tragedy and turn it into a ministry.

My family finally got to see me in the trauma ICU around one-thirty in the morning. Then a few of them camped out in the waiting room until they could see me again during normal visiting hours. Several of them slept on the floor that night. Over the next few days, they were able to get a room at UAB Towers to be able to sleep in something more comfortable than chairs or the floor. My mom also said they were shocked to see that the US marshals had sent flowers to me on Tuesday. She was so touched and shocked by their generosity. We learned that the US marshals always send something to a victim of a crime. It's their way of letting us know that we aren't alone and that they're here for us. The beautiful flowers had to stay in the waiting room because of ICU restrictions. I'm glad the flowers got to stay there for others to be able to enjoy them.

Most of my time in the ICU was a blur. Waking up in restraints was awful. There's no feeling, really, that can describe waking up and realizing you have a tube down your throat and your wrists are chained up in restraints. My first instinct was to yank that tube out of there, which of course explained the restraints!

I remember trying to open my eyes for the first time when I could hear Adam and my mom talking to me. Because of the tube, I couldn't talk, so I started trying to use sign language, which I had learned in college, to spell out words. They were trying to stay positive, but they quickly got frustrated and sad because I was trying to communicate with them, and they couldn't understand. Adam said he remembered them walking out of the room in tears because they didn't know what I was saying. In between visiting hours, my family shared with others in the waiting room about their sign language dilemma. One of my college roommates, Allison, looked up some sign language and made a copy of the alphabet for my family. They eventually figured out that I was trying to say, "Eyes," because I had some gunk in my eyes. I was so relieved when they wiped my eyes when they came back to visit me. They continued to talk to me, but I was so heavily sedated that I don't remember much. I do remember opening my eyes one time and seeing them at the door, putting on hats, gloves, and medical gowns to come see me.

The doctors and my family were amazed at how well I was doing in such a short period. They had fully expected me to be in the trauma ICU for at least five days. I would have to stay in the ICU until I no longer needed to be intubated. On Wednesday morning, I was doing well with breathing on my own, so they were able to remove my tube and restraints. That felt amazing! The first thing I asked the doctors was if I would still be able to have children. The doctors told me that none of the injuries affected my reproductive organs, so they were confident in the fact that I could still get pregnant in the future. I was so relieved. I was moved to the trauma/burn unit floor on Wednesday afternoon. This step-down room would allow more people to be able to visit me, and it would allow my husband to stay with me in my room!

I spent a lot of time sleeping those first few days. That was the only time that I wasn't in pain. There's really not a way to explain the pain of getting shot and then having exploratory surgery. I had over seventy staples vertically along my abdomen. I also had a chest tube, a nasogastric (NG) tube, a PICC (peripherally inserted central catheter) line in my neck, a JP (Jackson Pratt) drain, and another drain in my abdomen. Because the bullet went through and through, a nurse would have to pack the entry and exit wound. They would take long iodoform strips and carefully pack them into my wounds. The doctors said these wounds would heal from the inside out. Over time, the length of the packing strips got shorter as I began to heal. It was a very painful process that was very time-consuming because they had to do the packing slowly. I also had to take breathing treatments every few hours to keep my lungs healthy and have frequent X-rays and CT scans to monitor my healing. I also had the all-important morphine pump to help manage my pain. We would later find out that I am allergic to morphine. I got hot spots, red, rash-like patches in odd places all over my legs and arms. I was constantly hot, though I normally always feel cold. We kept the air in my room on the lowest temperature possible. I remember seeing people shiver at my bedside. Even Adam, who is hot-natured, would wear a fleece jacket in the room. I later had to apologize to some of my hospital visitors because I would ask people to take the sheets and blankets off me because I was so hot. My mom also bought me a yellow neck pillow that said *One Hot Chick*. She said it was perfectly fitting in that moment. I loved that pillow because it would help me sleep more comfortably on my back. I still sleep with that pillow today. It has traveled with me from Costa Rica to Alaska and everywhere in between.

I think my behavior started to worry my family as they got to spend more time with me in my step-down room. They said I would just stare off into space. I was never angry about what had happened to me, but I was confused. I was trying to make sense of things in my head. I no longer felt safe. I worried about people coming into the hospital to hurt me. All the perpetrators involved in my crime were captured less than twenty-four hours after my shooting, and Adam told me that they were all in jail. That did calm me, knowing they couldn't hurt me or anyone else. But what if one of their family members decided to settle the score? I had no idea that fear would stay with me for years before I learned to adequately cope.

By Friday, I was more alert and was talking more with my family and friends. My face was all over newspapers in Alabama. Adam had brought a copy into our room. He said the mug shot was in that issue. I told him that I wanted to see it. I was so terrified in that moment. What if they got the wrong guy? I looked at the tiny photo and breathed a sigh of relief. That was him. The officers did it. They found the right person. And now my perpetrator had a name: Keundre Lerico Johnson.

My family also held a press conference on Friday. They said news outlets had been calling all week long to get an update on me. My family chose not to do anything publicly until I was out of the ICU and improving more. Adam, my mom, and my mother-in-law met on one of the top floors at UAB Hospital for a press conference. Several TV stations and newspapers were there to hear about my progress.

The press conference was going to air on television that night at ten. Adam came by my bedside to talk to me about a few things before we watched the news together. He explained to me that he had wanted to make sure there was no way that people couldn't see Jesus when he spoke. He then sat down beside me and said, "Amy, you may hear some things I said that bother you. I told them that I forgave the guy for shooting you and that I know you will forgive him in your own time. I didn't want to rush you or upset you."

I looked at him with tear-filled eyes and said, "I forgave him when I was lying on the ground."

He began to cry as well, hugged me, and said he didn't know a time that he had been prouder of me.

Hospital Journey

My physical healing was quite the journey. Because of my injuries, I was given a sponge bath each day by a nurse or orderly. My nurses and doctors at UAB were absolutely amazing, but there was one orderly that still causes me to shudder. She was quite rough when she would bathe me and when she changed my sheets. Some other nurses/orderlies would push part of the sheets under me then pull from the other side. This lady would turn me almost completely on my side, stuff the sheet under me, then plop me back down. Then she would repeat the same thing on the other side. This made my pain skyrocket. It would also trigger a panic attack, though I had no clue at that time what was happening. After she would leave, I felt like I could never catch my breath. She would always wear metal bracelets that jingled. I could hear her coming and would cringe. After the second time she came to change my sheets, I told Adam and my mom that she couldn't come back again. I couldn't handle any more pain like that. He walked out to the nurses' station and very politely said that he and my mother could handle my sponge bath and change my sheets. He asked that the orderly not come back because of how roughly she handled me. Well, the next day, the orderly walked in, plopped the sheets down on the counter, and walked out. My mom and Adam took care of me from that point on. I never wanted to get anyone in trouble, but trauma patients need to be handled with extreme care.

My doctors and nurses were truly amazing. Dr. George told me that he was a little surprised to see that I was the patient that came in with a gunshot wound. He jokingly said that most people that come in with wounds like that don't normally have nicely manicured toenails or look so well put together. One nurse went out of her way to even take care of my feminine hygiene needs. I apologized to her about how sorry I was that she had to do that for me. She brushed it off like it was no big deal and said, "Honey, you have no clue about some of the stuff we see or do. This is nothing."

I thanked her again, but she seemed to be genuinely happy helping me. I tell this to brag on the UAB staff.

Sleep was hard in the hospital, not just for me but for Adam who stayed with me. Nurses were coming in around the clock to check vitals. Breathing treatments happened every few hours. X-rays were at five in the morning. I could sleep during the day, but I know it was hard on Adam because he didn't have that luxury. We constantly had visitors all throughout the day, so naps weren't possible for Adam. He never left my side for the longest time. After about a week, my mom suggested that he go stay at the UAB Townhouse to be able to get a full night's sleep and she would stay with me. Sleep was also hard for me because of my dreams. I would have very graphic, bloody, and disturbing dreams. I don't know if they were trauma-induced, a side effect of morphine, or a combination of the two. Sleep would free me from my physical pain but not from the mental anguish and confusion going on inside of me.

Walking for the first time was also a challenge in more way than one. The physical therapist, who came to my room, was a Black man that favored Keundre in build. I hated that feeling. I hated being afraid of someone for no legitimate reason. This guy was coming in here to help me. Why was I afraid of him? (This was part of a long journey of healing, which I will describe in a later chapter, when I went to counseling for PTSD.) Rodney was my therapist's name, and he was amazing. I added a picture at the back of this book of the two of us. I still had my chest tube and other drains that I had to maneuver in order to stand. Rodney gently helped me scoot to the edge of the bed, brought me a walker, and helped me to stand. My legs felt like they weighed a hundred pounds each at that moment. Then he wanted me to walk to the recliner, which was only about three feet away from my bed. I slowly made it to the recliner, and then he helped me turn around to walk back to my bed. Over the next few days, he increased the distance that I would walk. I made it to the hospital room door and, then would build up my stamina to walk down the hallway, dragging and carrying all my equipment with me. I remember my best friend, Kelly, walking with me down the hallway one day. I told her that my chest tube container was my juice box. She was not very amused at my choice of words, but my humor was returning!

The doctors required me to have CT scans every few days to monitor healing. I had to drink three glasses of contrast before each scan. The first time they brought me the contrast, my brother Andrew was in the room with me. They would mix the contrast with a lemonade-flavored drink to make it taste better. I told Andrew I was just going to drink them as fast as possible to get it over with. Bad idea. I had just finished about a cup and a half when I could barely get out. "Andrew, I need a—" Then I threw up every bit of contrast I had just chugged. I tried to warn him, but it was too late. My poor brother was just standing there in shock, trying to clean the mess off me since I could hardly move. He also called in a nurse to help get me new bedding and for us to find out what to do since I puked up a good bit of my contrast. (I didn't make that mistake next time!) The nurse told me to carefully drink the last cup of contrast and that it should still be enough for an adequate scan.

After a week or so in the hospital, I was finally going to get my chest tube taken out! The CT scans and X-rays showed that I no longer needed the chest tube to heal. I vividly remember the nurse coming in to talk about the removal. Any family members or friends in the room had to leave for this process. He explained that it would happen very quickly. He told me that I would have to breathe in, take a deep breath, and hold it. He would then yank out the tube and literally throw it across the room while he covered up the hole to keep out any germs or contaminants. He wasn't joking either. He flat out threw the tube, almost hitting the wall behind him. He sutured the hole and went on his way. I had some of the best sleep in over a week after that tube was out. I'm a side sleeper, so I had been forced to sleep on my back because of the chest tube. I still had the PICC line and other drains, but I could maneuver those and sleep on my side. I remember rolling over onto my right side, since the drains were on my left side, and sleeping like a rock. I slept so well that I woke up to a pile of drool on my pillow. Some of my college friends were sitting on the couch beside my bed when I woke up. I said, "I'm sorry, y'all, for the drool, but that was the best sleep I've had in ages!"

Around this same time, I was sitting up in bed, talking with Adam. I told him that I felt like there was something in my throat. I kept trying to cough it up, thinking it was phlegm or something. That wasn't cutting it. Maybe it was an ulcer or something. I stuck my fingers in my mouth and felt something in the back of my throat. I pulled out a tube from my throat! A nurse was in there when I did this, and I looked at her, and her face was in shock. She was like, "Ohhh. Hold on! Stop for a second!"

I explained to her again that I *knew* something was in my throat that was bothering me. She went to tell my doctor what I had done and asked what they should do now. The NG tube wasn't really doing much for me, so they said it could be removed properly. The problem with this? The thin tube had to go back down my throat then be pulled out through my nose for it to be removed properly. Oops. That wasn't very pleasant.

Keeping clean was another important thing for me. These sponge baths just weren't cutting it. I mean, I wasn't doing anything to get dirty, but I wanted my hair clean so badly. They had used dry shampoo and some other products that could wash my hair without water, but I never felt truly clean. After almost two weeks, I was able to walk to the bathroom and around the hallway. I asked my mom if it was possible for me to get my hair washed. This was on a Saturday, so the weekend nurses would change from week to week. She found a nurse and asked her if it would be possible, and the nurse said absolutely! She brought in a seat and set it inside my shower. The PICC line had been moved from my neck and was now in my arm. She got plastic wrap to cover the line to prevent water from getting on it or in it. They helped me take off my comfy pj's and put on a hospital gown. I sat on the seat and tried my best to tilt my head back. I had my other drains sitting in my lap. They wrapped a towel around my shoulders and started to carefully wash my hair. Even with all their provisions, my mom and that sweet nurse still ended up getting soaked. But they didn't care. That simple hair washing made me feel like a million bucks. I finally felt clean. I cannot remember the nurse's name for the life of me. But I do remember her deeds. I remember how much she cared about me. I remember that she was willing to go the extra mile for a patient. Just thinking about her still puts a smile on my face almost fifteen years later.

On this new floor, visitors were able to come during the normal visiting hours. I was also touched by the fact that my college professors came to visit me. It was such a kind gesture. It was wonderful getting to see more friends and family members. They were also able to bring in items for me. My room was soon adorned with balloons, flowers, and cards from so many people. My family taped to the walls many of the cards and drawings that people would send to me. It was so encouraging to me to see how many people cared and were praying for me. Complete strangers were sending me cards and well wishes. I still have every single card and drawing that was taped on my wall or mailed to me. It's a beautiful reminder of God's faithfulness and love in action.

The new visiting hours were great, except there was an age restriction on that floor. I had two nieces, Macee, then two, and Alyssa, eight. We were very close, and I spent a lot of time with them prior to my accident. They struggled with what was going on with their Aunt Amy. Another sweet nurse looked the other way when Adam asked her if they could bring in my oldest niece to see that I was okay. She knew that something was wrong with me, and my family knew it would help her if she could actually see me. I remember Alyssa coming to my bedside, and I assured her that I was okay and would be fine. Later that week, both of my nieces were at the hospital in the waiting room. I told Adam that I wouldn't mind walking down to the waiting room to see the girls.

I still had two drains in my left side. One of them developed a hematoma under it and would frequently bleed. I messed up several pairs of pajamas that had to be taken home and washed by visiting family members. When we walked out to the waiting room, I had pajamas on with a hospital gown wrapped around me. I sat down on a chair, and the girls were sitting in the row of chairs across from me. I could tell that they were both nervous but especially Macee. I definitely didn't look like their normal aunt. I had lost weight from not really being able to eat. My cheeks were sunken in, and I had gadgets and drains around me. I tried to talk to them about normal stuff and asked about things they were doing at home. We visited for several minutes when I started to get worried. That stupid hematoma was about to start bleeding again. I could *not* start bleeding in front of these girls, but how was I going to get out of there fast enough? I had all the stuff and walked slower than normal. I leaned over to Adam, who was sitting next to me. I told him that I felt like I was about to start bleeding and that we needed to leave as soon as possible. We told the girls that we had to get back to the room. I didn't even get a chance to hug them goodbye. I just knew we had to go pronto. I kept my arm covering that area on my stomach in case it did start to bleed. We had just barely made it out of the waiting room when blood soaked my pajamas and gown. We had a little trail of blood all the way back to my room. Adam went back a few minutes later to clean up the floor. One of the nurses told him that it wasn't necessary, but he said, "It's my wife's blood. I don't mind wiping it up."

It's not every day you hear that phrase. I'm just thankful the mess happened in the hallway and not in front of the girls. That drain was removed shortly after this incident because they realized it was no longer helping. I was one step closer to being free of all the extra equipment!

After over three weeks, my drains were all removed. My staples had been removed. I had been *so* nervous about having my staples out, worried about how much it was going to hurt. I told the nurse I was nervous, and they assured me it would not hurt. They were right. It just tickled. Honestly, I was worried over nothing! The PICC line in my arm was also taken out. My body was in the healing process. Things were progressing well. It was finally time to go home. I'll sleep so much better in my own bed. Bye, bye hospital! The doctors said I could continue healing at home—or so we thought.

Chapter 6

Time to Go Home

My mom and Adam helped pack up our belongings, and it was time to head home. I said goodbye to my nurses and doctors and thanked them for all that they had done for me. I was rolled out in a wheelchair and headed toward the parking deck. Adam had taken me for trips around the hospital in my wheelchair over the last few weeks. The walls had begun to cave in on all of us, so it felt like a treat to be rolled around the hospital to get a change of scenery. This trip was different. We were getting to leave! I'll also never forget that blast of August in Alabama heat when the automatic doors opened. Adam had pulled the car up close, and I was able to walk to the car.

It took us a little over an hour to get from UAB to our house. When we got closer to home, I saw balloons on our mailbox! As we went down our long driveway, I could see more balloons and decorations adorning our porch. What a sweet welcome home! Adam helped me out of the car and up the steps. I couldn't walk upright yet because of my incision. More balloons and flowers were inside of our house. And I realized my house was immaculately clean! My best friend, Ceje, and her mother-in-law had come over while we were in the hospital to take care of our house. They even rearranged my laundry room, which was awesome and more efficient than what I had done!

Adam stayed home for a few days before going back to work. I'm pretty sure we went home on a Saturday or Sunday. He wanted to make sure I was feeling okay before going back to work. Side note: Adam's boss at Traditions Bank was nothing but gracious to Adam.

When Tim Compton found out what had happened to me, he called Adam and told him to take all the time he needed to be with me. He even continued to pay Adam's salary throughout our hospital stay. How many bosses would do that? It's pretty amazing.

My mom and mother-in-law, Brenda, had a small notebook they kept at the hospital. They would list all visitors and when someone brought food, sent flowers, donated money, etc. They shared this information with me after we got settled in at home. I was in awe of the visitors and the generosity that was shown to my family. It was a very humbling feeling. I always knew that people were praying for us. I could feel the prayers, but I had *no* clue people had been giving financially. In hindsight, it made perfect sense. The majority of my family members and friends didn't live in Birmingham. They were driving here daily to visit me. They had to pay for parking. Adam and the others had to eat! Three weeks of meals were adding up. We even had someone send in a roll of quarters. How smart is that to be able to use it in the vending machines?

They also kept another notebook at home to help keep track of my medicine and when I could take pain medicine. Adam, Brenda, or my mom would write down the information for us to be able to take to the doctor on Wednesday, when I was scheduled for a checkup in the trauma clinic.

Things were going well at home until my mom started to notice I was becoming more reserved, lethargic, and less alert than I had been in the hospital. I was also starting to have more pain in my abdomen where the drains were removed. Adam had to continue to pack my bullet wounds and the drain holes. He dreaded doing this because it was becoming more increasingly painful with each day. I was lying on the bed one night for Adam to pack my wounds. The spot where I had, had the hematoma was swollen and beginning to harden. When he slowly pulled out the previous iodoform tape, it was discolored. I looked down at my abdomen and could see greenish gunk coming out from my wound. I knew this wasn't normal. I knew I must have an infection. We were going to the trauma clinic the next day, so Adam knew we would just tell Dr. George then.

As we were getting ready for my appointment the next morning, my mom took my temperature and discovered I had a fever. I vomited as well. Now they definitely knew something wasn't right. I found out later that my mom and Adam had talked about whether or not they should pack a suitcase for the appointment because they suspected I would be readmitted. They didn't want to scare me or discourage me, so they decided we would just go to the appointment as planned without extra provisions.

When we got to the trauma clinic, I still had a temperature. They did blood work to verify that I had an infection. They just didn't know where. The bullet had nicked my pancreas and should heal on its own. Was it that? Or was it the drain wound? Dr. George decided it would be best for me to be readmitted in order to do further testing. I was a little upset about the news, but I didn't mind much since I felt poorly.

Chapter 7

Spirit Renewed

Hospital stay number two began on August 23. During our previous visit, Adam asked me what I wanted to do with my car. I told him I never wanted to see it again. After my car was released from the police, a family friend took it to a dealership in Jasper to sell it. Then we started looking for other vehicles. That Altima had been so special to me because it was the first car I bought with my own money, but now it was just an emotional trigger. I was determined to get a vehicle and make it back to school in a few weeks. I missed the end of my summer semester classes. My professors sat down with my parents and told them that my grades were all As, and they would give me an A on my missed exams. Little did I know how hard my recovery would be physically and mentally. My hopes of making it back to school in a few weeks would not happen.

My former positive attitude began to dwindle during this stay. When you are in a situation like this, you have to try and make the best of it, or it will consume you. I previously had enjoyed a playful banter with my doctors, nurses, and residents. Even Dr. George said I had just the right amount of sass to be a pleasant patient. I would continue to pick with him and try to make him laugh, but I just felt discouraged. I was frustrated with this setback.

One positive aspect of this stay was that I didn't have drains, tubes, breathing treatments, etc. They continued to do frequent CT scans to monitor healing or to see changes. They also gave me IV antibiotics to help fight off the infection. I was more mobile, so we would take more trips around the hospital in my wheelchair. I was beginning to eat more as well. This was the first time in my life I ever needed to eat to gain weight! My family members were very agreeable to bringing me food whenever I was craving something I would actually eat. They just wanted me to eat something. My favorite treats were a few Chick-fil-A nuggets or a Meximelt from Taco Bell.

After several days in the hospital, they discovered that my pancreas wasn't healing well enough on its own. They noticed that my pancreas was leaking fluid into the rest of my body. This was the main cause of why I was feeling so poorly. They informed us that I would need another minor procedure to insert a drainage tube in my back for the excess fluid. More upsetting news was that I would have to leave the hospital with this drain still inserted in order for me to completely heal properly.

They set up a time for the procedure to be done the following morning. I would have a different doctor this time, instead of my beloved Dr. George. It must've been a busy day at the hospital because the morning hours continued to pass and I was still in my room, waiting. I was unable to eat anything before this procedure as well. I wasn't eating much in the first place, but I would still nibble a little bit. I was really starting to get hungry. Then the afternoon hours began to tick by with no procedure in sight. Adam went to ask a nurse for an update on the holdup. I was finally taken back for my procedure after five-thirty.

I was under local anesthesia, so I was in and out of sleep. Because this drain had to be placed in my back, I was required to be on my stomach the entire time. This was extremely painful because of my drainage scar holes and massive surgery scar. I hoped and prayed this wouldn't take long. As they were working, I heard a lady with an authoritative voice that sounded like she was in charge. Then I heard her say, "Well, I missed a really nice dinner because of this procedure."

I felt like, *Whoa, you've got to be kidding me*. I was trying to will myself awake to turn my head in her direction to say, "Lady, do you *think* I want to be here? I am so sorry you are missing your precious dinner because I got shot." But that didn't happen. I remember thinking it and then falling back asleep. It was still very upsetting. It's not like this was an elective surgery where I was getting work done to make myself look better. Sheesh. I guess that can be my PSA for doctors and nurses, who may be reading these. Please be careful what you say because you never know if your patient is awake or not. I know her words weren't intentionally said to hurt me, but they did. The procedure was completed successfully despite the unfortunate conversation.

We were nearing the end of August and still in the hospital. It was fairly late in the evening, and it was just Adam and me in the room. I asked him if I could see his Bible. I had heard about people reading a Proverb a day since there are thirty-one chapters and thirty-one days in the month, so I flipped over to Proverbs 30. I read it, and then something urged me to read Psalm 30 as well. This is what it said:

> *A psalm. A song. For the dedication of the temple.*
> *Of David.*
> I will exalt you, Lord,
> for you lifted me out of the depths
> and did not let my enemies gloat over me.
> Lord my God, I called to you for help,
> and you healed me.
> You, Lord, brought me up from the realm of the
> dead;
> you spared me from going down to the pit.
> Sing the praises of the Lord, you his faithful
> people;
> praise his holy name.
> For his anger lasts only a moment,
> but his favor lasts a lifetime;
> weeping may stay for the night,
> but rejoicing comes in the morning.
> When I felt secure, I said,
> "I will never be shaken."
> Lord, when you favored me,
> you made my royal mountain stand firm;

but when you hid your face,
I was dismayed.
To you, LORD, I called;
to the Lord I cried for mercy:
"What is gained if I am silenced,
if I go down to the pit?
Will the dust praise you?
Will it proclaim your faithfulness?
Hear, LORD, and be merciful to me;
LORD, be my help."
You turned my wailing into dancing;
you removed my sackcloth and clothed me with
    joy,
that my heart may sing your praises and not be
    silent.
LORD my God, I will praise you forever.

I cannot believe what I just read. I handed the Bible over to Adam with tears in my eyes and told him to read the passage. He read through it and began crying too. Then he looked at me and said, "You know it's not August thirty, right? It's the twenty-ninth."

Then I started crying even more. God has perfectly orchestrated this exact moment just for me. A nurse usually came in to write his or her name on my whiteboard, along with the date and other information. My board was completely blank that day. God used that to speak directly to me. I've never heard His voice audibly, but there is no doubt in my mind that He was speaking to my heart and spirit in that moment. Adam knew it too. He looked at me and said, "Get up. I want to dance with you."

We stood at the side of my hospital bed, weeping and slow dancing. It is one of the most precious moments I've ever had with him. Both of us needed that touch from the Lord.

I told Adam that I wanted some paper to write down the scripture. I wanted it plastered on my wall. He went to the nurses' station to ask for paper and a marker. I began filling these sheets with these God-breathed scriptures. He then got tape and hung the scriptures vertically down the wall in front of my bed. From that point on, my demeanor changed. I was no longer discouraged. I knew that God *was* going to turn my wailing into dancing. He spared my life for a reason. I would not be silent about His faithfulness Weeping may remain for a night, but joy comes in the morning! And two mornings later, we were released from the hospital for the final time!

C h a p t e r   8

Mental Battle

We were finally home for good, and my new reality was beginning to sink in. I had no clue how difficult the next year would be, but I was so happy to be in the comfort of my own home. Adam would also get to go back to work, and things would start to feel somewhat normal again. My new normal was an adjustment. My goal of getting back to school that semester was squashed. We had no idea about the severity of the physical restraints I would now have on my body.

Just a few weeks after our release from the hospital, one of my mom's friends, Wayne Brown, wanted to do something special for me. He organized a benefit concert, auction, and car show. I had never met this man before in my life, but he was putting all this together just for me! The news stations were there, and this would be my first opportunity to speak publicly about my trauma. Adam was sitting beside me, and my nieces were on my lap. I was still in shock that people would be so kind and caring to me. I shared that I was improving daily and looking forward to getting back to school. I thanked people for their prayers because that was what caried us through. Friends, family, and strangers all came together for this event. It was so touching. What's more, Wayne surprised me with a diamond-cluster ring. I was in shock and in tears. I gave him the biggest hug and thanked him for his unbelievable kindness in all he had done for me.

I was babysat for months. If Adam was at work, my mom or Brenda would be at the house with me. I kept all our blinds closed. I would get anxious every time I heard someone pull down our gravel

30

driveway. I lived in a constant state of fear. That was very frustrating to me because I've always been a people person. I was never shy growing up. I was always the kid that came home with new friends after a vacation. Now? I didn't trust anyone that I didn't already know.

I was healing faster physically than mentally. We still had to go to the trauma clinic for a checkup every Wednesday. They continued to do CT scans to make sure my drain was working correctly. The drain was placed near the middle of my back with a small tube that connected to a bag. I had an elastic strap to wrap around my waist so the bag would lay across my hip area. The drainage bag would have to be emptied and the tube flushed out several times a day. My helpers would also have to remove part of it for me to be able to take a shower. The drain was supposed to be able to hang from my back comfortably, but that wasn't the case with me. I always had to keep a large bandage across the tube to keep it from pulling on my skin. And the fluid coming out of it was gross. My husband deserves a medal for all the yucky medical stuff he had to do for me. That's when you know you've got the right one—they'll do whatever it takes in time of need. This drain would also give me trouble because the bag would get stuck inside a couch cushion. There were multiple times that I would get up from a couch and then quickly sit back down because the drain was stuck and yanking on my skin. I had to get used to that new normal and be more careful as I was getting up from a couch.

I was still having to take various medicines and painkillers. Helpers would write down the time I needed to take anything. Because I knew addiction ran in my family, I would avoid taking the stronger painkillers as much as possible. No one just says one day, "Hey, I would love to get hooked on painkillers." So I made sure that wouldn't happen. But because I did that, my physical pain was beginning to affect my mental health as well. I would get anxious as the pain increased. The pain honestly never went away at the hospital or at home. I had learned to cope with it. My mom informed me that they would not let me take any more medicine than what was prescribed and that I needed to stop hurting myself in this way. I needed to use the medicine not only to help curb the pain but also to ease my anxiety that would spike when the pain increased.

At one of my Wednesday appointments, I had talked with Dr. George about my anxiety. I didn't like this feeling of fear that would consume me. He diagnosed me with post-traumatic stress disorder (PTSD) and asked if I would like to take something for my anxiety. I began taking medicine for that periodically, when I would feel extra anxious or knew that I would be going out in public.

Anytime I would go anywhere in a car, I would immediately lock the doors. I still wasn't able to walk long distances, so I would use a wheelchair in a larger store or in the mall. I felt wiped out and drained just in the short distance from our car to the entrance of the trauma clinic or store. We were in the mall in Jasper several weeks after I was released from the hospital. I needed new clothes since most of mine no longer fit, and I wanted clothing with elastic over my abdomen. I was being pushed in the wheelchair when an older gentleman approached me and said, "Well, ma'am, why do you look so blue?"

I gave him a brief synopsis of my history and why I wasn't walking. He was just in shock. He had heard about my accident on the news and couldn't believe he was actually seeing me in person. He wished me well and hoped I had a swift recovery.

My mom and I were at Riverchase Galleria in Birmingham one day after a trauma clinic visit. I walked into the entrance with my arm in my mother's. She rented a wheelchair for me, and we went on our way. As we passed the food court, a man approached us and asked why I was in a wheelchair. When we had explained my story, he was taken aback. He was so apologetic. He worked at the mall and told us to come find him when we finished shopping because he was going to buy us lunch. (This next memory was one that I had actually forgotten about completely until my mom asked me about it.) We had finished all our errands and were ready to leave the mall. We retuned the wheelchair, and I was walking arm in arm again with my mom. As we were exiting the building, a Black man held the door open for us. I dug my fingernails into my mom's arm in fear. My mom thanked him for holding the door for us. When I got into the car, I burst into tears. My mom cried along with me because she knew I was struggling. I hated the person I had become. I hated judging people out of fear. That man didn't know me from anyone.

He was just being polite in holding the door for us. He was just being nice! (Since my mother had to remind me about this event, it shows me that God *really does* help heal our wounds in time.)

Adam and I also spent our first wedding anniversary with a drain in my back. We ate a year old freezer-burned cake and counted our blessings that I was still there to be able to celebrate a year of marriage! My mom jokingly said that we could write a book and title it *Carjackings, Shootings, and Burglaries: How to Survive Your First Year of Marriage*! I hope and pray no one else has this many crazy events to happen in their first year of marriage.

I helped teach a class of girls on Wednesday nights at church. Those sweet girls had diligently prayed for me and made me cards while I was in the hospital. I was so excited to get back into class with them. I didn't have enough stamina to teach them, but I was thrilled to just be with them and for them to see that I was okay. I told the girls that they could ask me anything if they were curious. My drainage bag would always garner looks, so it was no surprise they asked about it first. They had made a huge poster for me that said, "Welcome back, Mrs. Amy." I kept that poster up in our classroom for several weeks because it made me smile.

Adam and I were talking in bed one night, and I asked him to share details about his point of view from when he got the phone call, the ride to the hospital, etc. He also shared about how many people dropped everything to make it to the hospital. He started listing names upon names. Then I asked him if my dad was there. He got quiet and said no. He told me that no one in the family had planned on telling me about my dad's absence unless I directly asked. They were trying to protect me. And I completely understood why. I was heartbroken and devastated. People who didn't even know me personally were at the hospital to be there for my family members. But my dad didn't come? It was such a big hurt. He didn't like to drive at night, but he had more than one person volunteer to drive him. He brushed them off by saying, "She's not even going to know I'm there anyway."

He's right that I didn't know that night, but I knew now that he wasn't there. I just cried and soaked Adam's shirt with my tears. I couldn't even imagine how a father wouldn't do anything it took to get to the hospital for his child. But I knew why. That awful disease had taken over his brain to the point where he was no longer making good decisions. Before alcohol came into his life, I don't think a train or a lion could have stopped him from getting to me in the hospital. That heartbreaking decision was not my dad. That was not who he was. It was just another example of the painful effects of alcohol. Thankfully, my dad did come the next day and many times after that.

It was now mid-October, and I still had a drain. I still had company with me every single day. We had another clinic appointment with another CT scan. Dr. George told me that my scan looked good and my drainage output was continuing to get less and less. I would be getting my drain out that day! I had to lay on my stomach for this to be removed. Because of my incisions, this was still painful. He removed the drain then informed me that the entry would need to be cauterized. He began that process, and I was very quiet. He looked over at me and said, "Hello, Red. Are you okay? You're not talking or joking with me."

I gritted my teeth and told him it just really hurt. He apologized for my pain then bandaged me up. I had my mother take a picture of us together because I had no clue if I would get to see him again. This doctor had been such a huge part of my life over the previous months. We hugged and said our goodbyes, and I told him that I would be keeping up with him because he could never forget his favorite patient. I did stay in contact with Dr. George for several years before he moved to Ohio.

By this point, my scars didn't itch as much. I was told the itching was a normal part of the healing process. And wow, had they itched! It took me a while to even be able to walk upright because of my abdominal scars. I would look at myself in the mirror and wonder how Adam would still find me attractive. My body was riddled with so many scars. I didn't feel like I looked good. I had never worn a bikini in the first place, but those days were definitely out of the question now. But I still wanted to feel attractive to my husband. When I brought up my concerns to Adam, he told me that he had and always would love me and want me. He assured me that my scars didn't affect him at all. He said that if he does ever look at the scars, he is reminded of God's faithfulness. He's thankful for the scars because that means I'm still with him. His words of affirmation helped me realize that I was the only one having an issue with my scars. As of today, my scars have lightened up tremendously, and I no longer worry about how they look. They do end up making an interesting conversation whenever I go to a new doctor who doesn't know my medical history!

One afternoon, I decided to take a closer look at the cards people had sent me while I was in the hospital. My family had kept them all in several bags. I saw them on the floor in our basement and poured all of them out. I couldn't hold back tears as I was reading card after card from people that I didn't even know but who took the time to pray for me and send a card. My grandparents' church had their members write on cards every Wednesday night to send me. I even received an extremely heartfelt card from the mother of my high school boyfriend. The card that stuck out to me the most was one from a mother of a friend in college. Her name is Ms. Mann. The outside of the card said, "Everything that happens to a child of God is Father-filtered, and He intends to use it for good." Then the tears were flowing even more. I knew that God was going to use my story for His good. I still keep that card on my dresser as a daily reminder of God's goodness and faithfulness.

It was in November when I finally started to stay at home by myself. We didn't have an alarm system, but I continued to keep the blinds closed and doors always locked. Adam bought me a can of pepper spray to keep with me as well. I kept my home phone and cell phone near me at all times as well.

One afternoon, I decided it was time for me to take a bold step. I was going to walk to the mailbox. Our driveway was quite long, probably around 100 yards, so the trip would not be quick. I called Adam at work to tell him what I was about to do. I walked out the door and locked it behind me. I had Adam on the phone, my keys in between my knuckles, and pepper spray on the other hand. We live in a fairly secluded area, so people could've been hiding out in the woods to ambush me. I constantly fear retaliation from my perpetrators' families. What if they were waiting for this exact moment, when I was alone, to seek revenge? In reality, no one would actually do that, but that was how my mind was working in this moment. That's what trauma does to you. So I took a deep breath and walked off the porch and down the driveway. I periodically looked from left to right to check my surroundings. I reached the top of our driveway and got our mail. I turned around quickly to head back to the house. I walked into the house and locked the door. I breathed a sigh of relieve and felt exhilarated. I honestly felt like I had climbed Mount Everest. Adam said he was proud of me too. This was a huge deal for me and a major step in my emotional healing.

This event also helped me realize that my mental healing was going to take much longer than I thought and that I might need some help. I started seeing a Christian counselor at The Enrichment Center in Decatur. I would continue to see her for the next year. (You'll hear more about her later.) These counseling sessions were so instrumental in my healing. I used to think therapy was a crock, but, boy, was I wrong. Another blessing from this was that these sessions were monetarily compensated for me. Our family had no clue that the Crime Victims Compensation Commission was even a thing! Their mission is to lessen the financial burden on innocent victims of violent crime and to serve as a vehicle of hope for the rights of crime victims. They had reached out to my family while we were still in the hospital. We were told that any medical bills, counseling services, etc. that were paid out of our pocket would be refunded by them with proper receipts. We were not in a financial bind, but this surely was a blessing to help lessen the load of an already taxing ordeal.

We celebrated a wonderful Thanksgiving and Christmas with family. It's when you go through times of tragedy like this that it makes you count your blessings and cherish every minute you have with your family. We rang in the New Year at home, and then reality set in that I was going back to school. This meant driving back to Montevallo. Up to this point, I still wasn't driving at all, not with anyone else and definitely not alone. How on earth was I going to make it back to school? I was so confident months ago that I would make it back in a flash. Now my fear was crippling me.

For the entire month of January, Brenda (my precious mother-in-law) or my mom would drive me to school. Sometimes, Brenda would take me halfway and meet my mom, who would drive me the rest of the way. They never once complained. Brenda would sit out in her van during my classes. My classmates were thrilled to see me back. Since I had missed a semester, some of my friends were no longer in class with me since I was behind them now. Two of my good friends at school were Amy and Natalie. Amy and I were supposed to meet up at night the day I was shot to work on a project. That obviously never happened. The two of them came to visit me in the hospital. Amy came to my bedside and said, "Oh my goodness. I am so sorry that this happened to you. I don't know if you have your phone or not, but when you get it back, please just ignore the messages I left for you!"

I couldn't help but laugh. She was so apologetic about getting frustrated with me that I was leaving her hanging on our project. I told her that it was fine because, I mean really, who has a classmate that gets carjacked and shot just a few hours after you've seen her? My phone was eventually recovered from where it had been dumped. I giggled as I listened to her messages. Sadly, Amy and Natalie were no longer in classes with me.

I took another leap of faith in February. I was going to drive by myself to school. Well, sort of. My mom or Brenda would follow behind me in their own vehicles. I did this for a few weeks then I decided I would drive alone halfway there and my mom would follow me to Montevallo for a few days. Slowly but surely, I got up enough confidence to make the trip by myself. It was definitely a struggle, but I knew it was a step I needed to take. One more mission accomplished!

Next hurdle—facing my perpetrators for the first time.

Chapter 9

The Reckoning

There were three people involved in my carjacking and shooting. Multiple police departments were involved in my case as well as the US Marshals. I was abducted in Homewood and shot in Hoover. My car was dumped in Vestavia Hills, and my phone was found in Leeds. Keundre was the one who held me at gunpoint and shot me as I jumped out of the car. He had recently turned eighteen. His cousin, Mackese Walker Speight, was driving the vehicle that followed us. She was twenty-eight and a mother of two children. There was also a seventeen-year-old boy involved.

All three pled guilty to being involved in my crime. Keundre and Mackese had been on a crime spree before they abducted me. They committed armed robbery at a subway on July 26 around 6:00 p.m. Then they placed an order for pizza to be delivered to a hotel with a phony room number. Around ten, the delivery man went into the hotel to find this room. Upon returning to his car, he was held at gunpoint and robbed. They made this man get into the passenger seat of their car and drove off with him. After a few minutes, they brought him back to his vehicle and ordered that he get down on the ground and not move or he would get shot. And what's crazy was that Keundre even took the pizzas from the victim's vehicle.

On July 27, they committed armed robbery at a Cicis Pizza. On July 28, they robbed another subway at gunpoint. They shot at a bystander, who was standing outside the restaurant, looking in their direction.

July 31, they were able to get into my sister's gated apartment complex because the gate was left open during busy hours. They saw another person to carjack but saw a car seat in that vehicle, so they skipped over it. I was their next choice. They carjacked and shot me and left me for dead. They dumped my car into the overflow parking lot at Shades Mountain Baptist Church. They sent the seventeen-year-old to wipe down my vehicle. The federal attorney later said, concerning sending a seventeen-year-old NOT involved in the crime to wipe down the crime scene. "If criminals weren't so dumb, our jobs would be really hard." He said that in the courthouse—I think before all of the sentencings. It didn't work—his fingerprints were on my vehicle in multiple locations. Just a few hours later, they carjacked another woman at a car wash. They put this woman in the trunk shortly after leaving the car wash. They eventually took her out of the trunk and ordered her to tell them how to get to the closest bank. This lady got them $60 out of an ATM and managed to escape as another customer pulled into the parking lot. Mackese went toward this new lady and demanded money. She quickly got back in her car and fled but not before Mackese fired at her and hit her driver's door and headrest.

I tell you all this to let you know I wasn't their only victim. I may have been the only victim with physical injuries, but these others would surely struggle with the mental aspect of being a victim of a crime. Your safety and security have been taken from you. Your life will never be the same.

On September 27, 2006, a federal grand jury returned a seven-count indictment against Mackese and Keundre. They were charged with one count of conspiracy to commit carjacking, three counts of carjacking, and three counts of using a firearm during a crime of violence. Keundre pled guilty on all charges. On October 12, Mackese entered a plea of not guilty to all counts at her arraignment. A trial was set for Monday, February 12, 2007. Four days before trial, she withdrew her plea and entered a blind plea to the charges against her. Since both of my perpetrators pled guilty, we would not have to go to trial. This was such an answered prayer for me. I was dreading having to relieve every detail of my accident. I don't mind sharing my testimony with others but going through every detail in a court-room? That was terrifying. That was one load off my shoulders, but it wasn't over. I still needed to see them face-to-face at their sentencing. The seventeen-year-old was tried as a juvenile and received a shorter sentence. I felt like he was just in the wrong place at the wrong time and got roped into these crimes. He had also been deceived to go with them on the 31st, as he had been promised some money for moving furniture and something to eat. He had no idea what was going on. When asked by the attorney if he got anything for moving furniture, he said no. He was asked if he got anything to eat, he said, "No, not even a happy meal." as people in the courtroom laughed.

On April 26, 2007, my family and I went to Keundre's sentencing. I was able to do a victim impact statement, going before the judge and explaining how this crime has affected me, my family, etc. US attorney Bill Simpson represented me in every case. He did a wonderful job of preparing me for how it would look and go. He and Adam told me that there would be uniformed guards bringing in Keundre and that he would be in handcuffs, ankle chains, and wearing a taser belt. One US marshal in the room had the remote to the taser belt. They also told me there would be additional US marshals in civilian clothing throughout the courtroom. That helped calm my nerves a little because I felt very protected. We had attended their arraignments prior to this, so I wasn't as nervous about seeing them since I had already tackled that hurdle. What did terrify me was how close I would be to the man who shot me. We had sat in the back for the other court visits, where my family would have me comfortably squished among them. Today? I had to walk right past him and stand with my back to him. I was shaking like crazy, but I knew I *had* to do this. Why was this so important to me? I wanted him to see what God can do. I wanted him to see the power of the God I serve. I knew I would probably never get a chance to speak to him if I didn't do it then.

I walked up and stood before the judge. Attorneys were flanked to my left and right. I proceeded to tell the judge how long I was in the hospital, about the drain I had to keep in my back, how I had to delay school for a semester, how I no longer felt safe in my own home, etc. I explained how this ordeal has impacted my friends, my family, and my community. Then I turned and looked Keundre straight in the eyes. I told him that I forgave him after he shot me and that I was praying he would find forgiveness with the Lord. It became another moment where God took over and walked me through. Right after I told him that I forgave him, it was the first time I ever saw a glimmer of remorse on his face. I hope he could see Jesus in me. One of our assistant attorneys hugged me and spoke to me after the sentencing. She said she has never cried at a sentencing before that day. Her words were a blessing to me because it reminded me that God can use my story to make an impact on our legal team as well.

When I came in and walked to the stand, there was a good bit of movement in the courtroom. It was all the plain clothed US Marshals, moving to strategic spots to protect me if needed. After the sentencing was over, Mr. Simpson told Adam that this was the most US marshals he had seen in a courtroom since the case of Eric Robert Rudolph. Why? Keundre was reported to have been running his mouth in jail about something "big" was going to happen that day. They took extra precautions just to be on the safe side. I know I definitely felt better knowing I had so many people to protect me.

Mackese had her sentencing on May 24. They both had state and federal charges. Between all those charges, they were sentenced to sixty-eight and seventy-one years in prison without parole. They were automatically given seven years for brandishing a firearm. If a gun was brandished another time, it was twenty-five years. They were both slapped with fifty-seven years just in gun charges. My mind could be at ease now, knowing that they would not have the ability to hurt anyone else.

At Mackese's sentencing, her parents were there. Her mother was a retired teacher and her father an elder at their church. She didn't come from a broken home but the exact opposite. She was raised in a loving, godly home. My family was allowed to exit the courtroom first, while her family had to stay. We made it down the elevator and outside of the court building. We were discussing where to go eat lunch when Mackese's parents approached us. Her mother asked Adam if it was okay to talk to me. He asked me, and I said yes. She gave me a huge, genuine hug and just kept apologizing for what had happened to me. She said just couldn't figure out where she had gone wrong for her daughter to have done it. She said they would've given her money if she needed it. Her parents were clearly upset because they were basically losing a daughter because of her actions. Yes, they could still visit her in jail, but it would not the same. They were grieving and hurt—just like the victims of the crimes. My heart was truly breaking for her parents. Then Mackese's ex-husband walked up to us and shoved a picture of their children in my face. He said, "These kids won't have a mother now."

I looked at Adam and told him that I needed to leave. That tender moment I had with her parents was ruined in seconds. That picture of her children still haunts me today. I can still see them in my head.

After the sentencing, I went to another counseling session fairly quickly to help me deal with my emotions. I told my counselor what the ex-husband had done to me and how much I was struggling with it. I told her that I felt guilty because the children would be growing up without a mother because of me. She did a wonderful job of explaining to me that I was taking ownership of something that I didn't do. She told me that if I was going to take ownership of *that*, then I needed to take ownership of the fact that I probably saved someone's life because they were in jail. That finally sank in. I knew deep down they would possibly have killed someone if they had continued with their crime spree. She also helped me to understand the importance of forgiving him. Forgiving him set me free. It showed that he didn't have control over me. Yes, I was a victim of a crime, but it didn't mean I had to stay a victim. If I had stayed a victim, he would have won. He would have control. We need to forgive, even if the person never asks for it, even if the person never regrets what they've done. The person that it frees is *you*. We cannot hold the banners of victim and victory at the same time. I heard a pastor say recently that forgiveness is a choice, not a feeling. When we forgive, we are refusing to be locked in a bond of bitterness, hatred, and resentment for the rest of our lives.

She also helped me cope with my new normal. I was very frustrated with myself when things weren't going back to normal as quickly as I had hoped. I shared that I hated the way I would judge people out of fear. That wasn't like me. I used to talk to anyone and everyone. She told me that I was measuring myself to last year's Amy—pre-trauma Amy. That was not the same person. She helped me understand that it was unfair and unfeasible to hold myself to the same level before my shooting. I wasn't the same person as before, so I shouldn't hold myself to that standard and beat myself up. It felt like a ton of bricks were lifted off my chest. She also reminded me that some of these fear-driven behaviors would be temporary and subside over time. And she was right. She also helped me identify my PTSD triggers and how to cope with them. One obvious trigger was loud, sudden noises, which was kind of strange to me because I never heard the gunshot or felt it as I was jumping out. I literally had no clue I had been shot until I looked down at my shirt. Another trigger was the smell of freshly cut grass. Someone must've cut grass close to where I jumped out. This trigger has gotten better with time. Being hot also triggers anxiety. I was hot in the hospital from the morphine allergy, but I was also extremely hot when I was on the ground after being shot. It was July 31 in Alabama. It was hot. This is one trigger that will still rear its ugly head from time to time.

Throughout all of this, God has been faithful. There is no doubt in my mind that He was in the car with me, guiding my steps. He showed me a safe place to jump out. He let me see angels that day. He spared my life. I must proclaim His good deeds. Jesus died for my perpetrators just as much as he did me. None of us deserves His mercy and grace, but praise God. He is a loving God. He is the only reason I am able to share my story. Because of this event, I have been given the opportunity to share my testimony at churches and ladies' events. He gave my family and me that peace that passes all understanding. He gave us strength to stand. He carried us when we couldn't walk. He wrapped His loving arms around us to comfort us in one of the most terrifying times in our lives. He predestined this to happen to me. I have often wondered, why me? Then I thought, why not me? I deserve nothing. But I do know that God prepares

His people in advance. Adam and I had no clue on our wedding day what we would be enduring in the next year. What we did know was that God will never leave us or forsake us. We knew that His ways are higher than ours. We knew that He works *all* things out for good. And our story isn't over yet with what God can do. It's only just beginning.

Life Adjustments

On April 16, 2007, my breath felt taken out of me. I was attending class when I heard about the shooting that took place at Virginia Tech. I was terrified, but my classmates were so comforting to me. I began looking around the classroom for a possible place to hide if anything like that happened to us. My anxiety was in high gear, making it difficult to breathe. I vividly remember where I was sitting in class my senior year when I heard about the Columbine shooting in 1999. Yes, I was scared then as well, but it was nothing like what I was experiencing that April day. Just as I was starting to get more courage to get back to normal activities, this happened and set me back a few steps.

July 31, 2007, was the first anniversary of my shooting. I was filled with anxiety and on edge in the days leading up to this. I was also dealing with some unexplained shoulder pain. I talked with Dr. George about the pain, and he referred me to another doctor at UAB. I was at the doctor on July 31 for an ultrasound to see if they could get to the bottom of my pain. The doctors were thinking I could have gallstones. Once they completed the ultrasound, a little string of pearls showed up in my gallbladder, and so another surgery was scheduled to remove yet another organ. It was strange to me that I had always been healthy prior to my incident, and now I had gallstones. The doctors did say gallstones can form as a result of trauma to the rest of the body. My surgery was scheduled a few weeks later.

My family spent time with me after my doctor's appointment to celebrate another year of life and to celebrate God's provision and protection. The next few weeks were filled with flashbacks of where I was just a year prior. I was glad that I was still in school because that would occupy my thoughts, instead of me revisiting the past. My gallbladder surgery went successfully. I only missed two days of school and went back on a Friday. We had a field trip that day, so Brenda drove me to school. My classmates were furious that I had come to school that day! In the education program, you were only allowed one or two absences before they docked you a letter grade. I wasn't about to get a B because of a surgery. I made it around American Village just fine.

Another change that happened during this time regarded singing. I had always enjoyed being on stage at church in our local theater growing up or in our theater program in high school. I liked being part of the crowd on stage, but I rarely wanted a solo. The idea made me so nervous. My brother-in-law, Brad, was involved in chorus, growing up, and sang in church. Adam also sang in church. They wanted the three of us to start singing together. I was terrified. I only sang harmony with them during the first song we sang at church. I kept making excuses about not singing by myself. I was too worried about messing up or my voice cracking while I tried to reach a note beyond my range. After several months of running from this, I felt God speak to my heart. He told me that I needed to stop worrying about what other people thought and just sing for Him. He told me that He spared me for a reason and I needed to sing His praises. So I stepped out in faith the next time we sang. Adam's father was our choir director at church, and he had also asked me to sing a solo at church. I struggled through the song because it spoke so closely to my heart. The words began with "When I am in trouble, where does my help come from? I look unto the hills whence cometh my help. I trust in God. I know He cares for me." I had experienced those exact words. My help came from the Lord when I was in the midst of danger. I truly enjoy singing with Adam and Brad now. I also sing in our praise band at church, and I am thankful to be able to still be here to sing His praises!

Fast forward to May 2008—graduation day! I was so excited to be finished with school and begin the career that I knew was perfect for me! I spent that summer joyfully on the job hunt. I dropped off my resume and portfolio at several different school systems. The entire month of June went by with no bites. Then I heard about a possible job opening right down the road from Adam's work, and it was where he had graduated. I loved the idea of a small-town school. I interviewed for a fifth-grade position. I knew this job would possibly only last for a year, but I was excited at the opportunity. I was later called and offered the job. And guess what day the offer came? July 31. I just cried to the principal on the phone and told her that I couldn't believe I would get offered a job on that day! That's just what God does. There's 365 days in a year. He chose that specific day to lift my spirits, to remind me that He's still in control. Now I had just a few weeks to get ready for the first day of school!

Since I had a job now, Adam and I were finally going to start trying to have a baby! My ob-gyn doctor was aware of my accident, and he told me to actively try for three months. I was tracking my ovulation for three months, and we were not pregnant. So Dr. Edwards told me to come in for some testing. They did an exam and took some blood to check for anything that might be an issue on that end. My blood work came back normal, so the doctor told us to continue trying for another three months before coming back.

It's often in these good times that we can take our eyes of Christ. I was happy to have a job, and we were going to start a family. Life felt good. I lost focus of the one who was in charge. But from this, I would be reminded of the beauty of our relationship with Christ. He's always waiting with open arms to take us back. He's the one that never moved in the first place! If you feel distant from God right now, look inward and see who moved. It's not Him. He's waiting for you to return. The hardest part of this now is forgiving ourselves for when we stray. When the Bible says He casts our sin as far as the East is from the West, He means it. Think about a globe. There's a defining mark that separates the northern hemisphere from the southern hemisphere. But what about east and west? There is no boundary. His forgiveness is forevermore! We always seem to press into Jesus when times are hard. I needed to remember to do the same when times were good.

We continued trying to get pregnant for another three months with no luck. I was now sent to do another ultrasound to check my ovaries and see if I was having issues with my eggs. The results would show that my eggs were not fully maturing. Another surprising finding was that I had almost no eggs on my left ovary and very few on my right. The majority of the trauma to my body was on the left side. I didn't think this was a coincidence, but the doctors couldn't definitively say that this was a result of my accident. All hope was not lost in me conceiving a child though! I would take some hormones to help the eggs mature and then possibly try in vitro fertilization (IVF) if I couldn't get pregnant on my own. But the doctor was still concerned that we weren't pregnant after six months, so he wanted some testing done on Adam as well. I'm glad I got shot, as it means Adam doesn't bear the burden of infertility alone.

I went with Adam to his doctor's appointment in April 2009. I wanted to hear what the doctors were saying to him about our chances of conceiving. He had testing done and blood work taken as well. Within less than an hour, our lives would be turned upside down again. We received devastating news about our ability to conceive. Now it would require shots, surgery, recovery, lots of money, and that was only for a 10 percent success rate. This was another one of those moments where God gave us strength in our time of need.

Adam and I held it together in the doctor's office, but Adam broke down once we got back into the car. He was heartbroken over us not being able to get pregnant. I think he hurt for me as well because he knew I had always wanted to carry a child. I couldn't wait to be pregnant. In that moment, God allowed me to be a rock for Adam. He had been so strong for me years ago, and now it was my turn. I had an overwhelming peace. I wasn't crying at all. I looked at Adam and said, "Okay, that's it. Let's look into adoption. We know we are supposed to be parents, so this may be the avenue we are going to take to get there. We know who is the giver and sustainer of life. If *He* wants us to have a child, He's going to open my womb and make it happen. Let's start researching agencies." I seriously couldn't believe how strong God allowed me to be in that moment.

I wish I could say I stayed strong, but it just wasn't true. In the coming weeks and months, I've kept this struggle private. I wanted to protect Adam from my hurt. I was also back on the job hunt again. I knew, going into my teaching position, that it could possibly be for just one year, but it still hurt to be let go! Now I have no job and no child. I called the summer of 2009 my dark summer. I have no clue that I was battling depression during this time. I sat around the house and didn't want to do much of anything. I was having a good little pity party for most of my summer. I was not even looking for a job in earnest, like I had been the year prior. It was another time in my life when I felt completely alone. I felt alone when I was in the hospital because I didn't know anyone else that had been carjacked and shot. I had no one to talk to, no one to relate with. I again felt alone in my infertility struggle. In my mind, I knew I was not the only who was going through this, but I personally didn't know anyone walking this same journey. Some days, you just need someone to talk to that's experienced what you are experiencing. It was such a lonely and dark time in my life. I feel paralyzed by my grief.

Some people may think it's crazy to say I was experiencing grief. I didn't lose anyone. But I did lose what could be, what could become. I had always looked forward to becoming a mom and being pregnant. I looked forward to every aspect of it. I lost the dream of carrying a child. I lost the dream of experiencing a baby kick for the first time. I lost the dream of my husband kissing my growing belly. I lost the dream of purchasing maternity clothes. No one would be doting over me as I carried a child. I wanted to experience all of it—the delivery, the stretch marks, you name it. I wanted it. I basically used that summer to grieve my loss, yet I couldn't bring myself to get rid of some maternity pieces I had bought for myself. I kept hoping for another miracle. If you are reading this and thinking, "That's me," please know you're not alone. I am sorry that this road of infertility is one you must travel. I think people have a hard time understanding this pain. The only way I can explain it is to acknowledge that I would rather experience the physical pain again of getting shot than have someone tell me I may never carry a child.

I was unable to find a teaching position the next year, but I did get hired as an aide. This allowed me to keep my insurance and pursue adoption in earnest. Adam and I had started researching agencies locally and around the US earlier in the summer. We found an agency in Florida that we really liked. We started the long and arduous process. We had to fill out pages of paperwork, get a home study completed, be interviewed multiple times, and (the fun part) create a profile book. I'm pretty creative, so I was excited about getting to make the profile book for birth mothers to get to learn more about us. It's basically a scrapbook full of pictures and information about yourselves. We included details of how we met, pictures of our wedding, tidbits, like our love of travel and our hobbies, and the explanations of why we wanted to become parents and why adoption. The list went on and on. I got the book finished and mailed it to Florida. Our home study was completed in September. So now we were just praying we would get chosen quickly!

―――――――――――――

Chapter 11

―――――――――――――

Adoption Struggle

We were so excited to be finished with all the work up front when it came to adopting. Now it was just a waiting game and praying hard for a baby. I began buying small things here and there that were gender neutral. I mean, we could get a phone call any time about a baby. We needed to be prepared!

We had an interview with a birth mother in October. Since the agency was in Florida, we had to interview over the phone or via Skype. This interview went well, but we were not picked for this baby. It was a few more months before we would get to be interviewed again. The months kept moving along, but we were still without a child. I kept thinking I needed to change something in our profile book. *We have a cat. What if they don't like cats? What if they like dogs better? Maybe they didn't like something else I put in our book.* I was constantly second-guessing everything within our profile book. I was so desperate for a child that I was willing to change some parts about me in our profile book. All this time, I was giving this to God. I kept telling Him that I knew it was in His hands, but I was the one trying to fix things and make an adoption happen.

I struggled a lot during this time. I was tired of rejection. I was tired of seeing pregnant women. Now don't get me wrong, every child is a gift from God—it just hurt so much to be constantly reminded of what I couldn't do, to see reminders of what I yearned for. I would find myself envious of women that I saw with babies or those currently carrying a child. Then God almost smacked me in the face one day and said, "How do you know what they've been through? What

51

if they've been trying IVF for years, and this was the one that finally worked?" God showed me the error in my thought processes.

What may seem well-meaning could be extremely hurtful to someone like me. Once, a mother shoved her teenage daughter's baby in my face and said, "It's your turn to have one!" She had no idea of the journey we were on. Another time, when we shared that we were going to adopt, a lady told me that this was great since I would be getting off easy because I wouldn't have to deal with childbirth. Are you kidding me? I'm getting off easy? Nothing about this was easy. It was the hardest thing I've ever had to deal with. I even had another seasoned lady at church come up to me, put her hand on my belly, and tell me that God was going to bless my womb. I'm not telling you all this to speak badly of these ladies. They are wonderful, God-fearing women. But I am sharing it to help make us aware of the power of our words. We may never know the silent battles people are facing, so we need to speak words of life and encouragement.

My dad also started to have more medical problems during this time. He was eventually admitted into the hospital. He was diagnosed with chronic obstructive pulmonary disease (COPD) and had cirrhosis of the liver. He was also dealing with congestive heart failure. Adam and I went to visit him in the hospital. He was in pretty bad shape, so I wanted to make sure I saw him. I had held onto so much hurt from him not being at the hospital the night I was shot. I stood by my father's bedside and told him that I forgave him for not being there. I told him that it hurt me greatly but that I wasn't going to let that hinder me anymore. I needed to forgive him in order to free myself. He was emotional and apologized for not being there for me or my family. I told him that I loved him very much and knew that he would do anything for me but that his disease had taken over his body so he could no longer think clearly. My siblings and I had shared with him before about how his decisions in life affected us, but I wanted him to know that I forgave him. If he wasn't going to make it out of this illness, I didn't want him to die without knowing my heart.

Mother's Day was always so hard. I 100 percent wanted to honor my mother, grandmothers, and the other important women in my life. But it was a painful reminder of what I was not. In church, they would ask all the mothers to stand and be recognized. And there I was sitting, alone and in my pain. I was at church with my mom this year in Decatur. I could tell she could sense the pain I was feeling, as it was very hard for me to hold back my tears. Before they recognized the mothers, they had a family come up and share a bit of their testimony. They, too, had been wanting to grow their family. God knew I needed to hear what they had to say. They referenced the story of Job. Job 1:21 (CSB) states, "…The LORD gives, and the LORD takes away. Blessed be the name of the LORD." I tried too hard to hide this in my heart. I so desperately wanted to believe this was true, but I was struggling.

One positive in the middle of our waiting was that I got a teaching job in Jasper. It was a new school to me where I didn't really know anyone, but I was so excited to have my own classroom again. I spent the summer getting my classroom ready and trying to somewhat prepare a nursery just in case. The busyness was a nice distraction from the waiting. A neat experience during this time occurred when I was coming home from Decatur one day. It had been a while since I had shared my testimony anywhere. I started praying in the car that God would give me another opportunity to share what He had done in my life. I kid you not—my phone rang about thirty seconds after I had voiced that prayer. It was a call from a church, asking me if I could come share my testimony. That was the one and only time in my life that I knew God had immediately answered a prayer.

July rolled around, and we had a birth mother interested in us! We would have an interview with her on *my* birthday! I was so excited because God loves to use special dates. He gave me a job on the anniversary of the day I got shot. Surely, He will let me find out that I'm going to be a mother on my birthday!

Nope. It didn't happen. She went with another family. And let me tell you—you think it felt bad to be picked last on a team in elementary school? This was a thousand times worse. I thought, *We are pretty good people. Why wouldn't someone pick us?* But we kept going up and down on this roller coaster of emotions. My hopes get high when we have an interview, and then they are quickly crashed when we hear another no. And again, I started thinking of what I could do to change this. *What can I do to make this process go faster so someone will actually pick us?*

School started in August. I was so happy to be teaching a group of fifth graders this year. I was up front with my principal about us being in the adoption process and not really knowing when we would get chosen for a baby. I was so worried about it being my first year at a school and then having to leave suddenly for a maternity leave. Well, that was one bridge I was willing to cross! I just wanted to be a mother, and school could wait. The entire month of August passed by with very little promise of a child.

It was now around mid-September, a Sunday at church. I honestly couldn't tell you a word of what my pastor was saying, but God completely got hold of me. I've never heard His voice audibly, but I knew He was speaking to me. It finally sank in what I was doing. I kept saying that I was giving this adoption to Him, but I would pick it right back up a day later or, sometimes, even a few hours later. I went down to the altar and cried out before Him.

I said, "God, I am so sorry. I am sorry for thinking that I know better than you. I'm sorry for trying to fix things on my own. Please forgive me. God, I am laying this completely at your feet once and for all. I can't do this anymore."

Tears were rolling down my face. I felt like a brick has been lifted off my chest. Then I heard God speak to my heart: "Amy, this is what I wanted from you all along. I never meant for you to carry this burden alone."

I started sobbing even more, but I felt free. I felt peace. I felt joy for the first time in a long time. I had no idea that this complete surrender would be the catalyst for change in just a few short weeks.

Chapter 12

God Shows Off

Just a few weeks after I had fully and completely surrendered our adoption, I got an email from my cousin Alison. She told me that she was teaching with a lady, Lee Ann, whose daughter was expecting and was looking for a Christian couple for adoption. Alison enthusiastically told Lee Ann, "Yes! My cousin and her husband are trying to adopt. I think this would be great."

I was joyously optimistic by this out-of-the-blue encounter. I quickly called Adam to tell him about this news so we could make this a matter of prayer. Alison was wondering if we had a profile book or anything she could send Lee Ann. Our hard copy of the profile book was in Florida, so I had to see if they could scan it for us. The agency agreed, scanned our information, and emailed it to me. I sent it to Alison, who sent it to Lee Ann.

Lee Ann and I begam to correspond with each other through emails off and on. She said that she, her daughter, Patricia, and her husband, Henry, enjoyed looking through our profile book and wanted to meet in person. Oh my goodness. I was thrilled but extremely guarded. We had, had our hopes up before, so I wasn't going to get worked up this time. We all agreed to meet at Cracker Barrel on October 23. Patricia was seriously the cutest little pregnant lady ever. We had a wonderful lunch and really seemed to hit it off. It didn't feel forced or fake. We found out that she was due in February with a boy. (I was secretly disappointed because I was really hoping for a girl. Girl clothes are so cute!)

As we were talking, Patricia shared that she loved all our profile book. Remember all those times I wanted to change stuff in our book in order to get picked? Yeah, God took care of that. I like cats. Patricia loves cats. I like baking. She likes baking. I was so giddy inside because I felt like God was saying, "See? I told you so. Just trust me!" We finished our meeting and went outside. We took a picture with Patricia on a bench outside of the restaurant. We hugged and said our goodbyes.

I will never forget being at that red light outside of the restaurant. My heart was racing. This just felt right. But I was so scared. Previously, we had asked lots of people to pray when we had a birth mother meeting, and it was so painful to have to share with them that we weren't picked. We had only told our closest family members about this meeting. We prayed at the red light for God to have His way in this situation. We didn't even tell many people that we were going to meet with the family. This way, we wouldn't have to deliver disappointing news to as many people.

We went to church the next day. Adam was leading worship. We went home and took that all-important, God-glorified Sunday afternoon nap. We had church that evening, had dinner, and then we were just relaxing in the living room. Adam was watching TV, and I decided to check my emails. I looked at my work email and saw that I had an email from Lee Ann. The first line said, "We really enjoyed meeting with you, guys, yesterday. Patricia said you, guys, need to start deciding on a boy's name—" I couldn't read anymore! I couldn't believe it. We were going to get a baby! I immediately got up off the couch and headed to the bedroom. I had bought a little Dad Guardian Angel car statue that I had planned to give Adam to tell him that I was pregnant. Well, that didn't happen, so I could give it to him now to tell him that we were going to be parents! I walked back into the living room and handed it to Adam with tears in my eyes. He just looked at it and at me, confused. Then I said loudly, "She picked us!"

We hugged and cried together. Then we wanted to go share the news with someone! It was after eight-thirty at this point, but we couldn't keep this to ourselves. We got in the car and headed over to his parents' house, which was practically in our backyard. We also stopped at his brother's house to tell them. He told us when he saw the headlights coming down their driveway that he knew we were getting a baby. But how was I going to tell my parents? This is too important to just say over the phone.

My parents both live an hour away from us, so I knew this wouldn't happen that night. I would have to sit on this exciting news until after school. I found a cute baby onesie that said, "What happens at Grandma's house stays at Grandma's house." We made up some excuses as to why we would be in Decatur. It was pretty close to Halloween, so I told her that we were going to stop by and give her a happy for Halloween. It wasn't uncommon for us to give each other random gifts, so I didn't think she suspected anything. She was sitting in a recliner in the corner of their living room. I walked in and gave her the gift. She opened it up, read it, and started crying. She was thrilled. This little boy was going to make her a grandparent for the first time! I told her that she needed to keep this news quiet until we could tell more people in person. We left her house to go tell the news to my dad. He was excited to finally be a grandpa. Throughout the next week, we would continue to share our big news with friends and family. We also asked them to continue to pray because adoptions could change in an instant.

Next, we had to figure out a name. This was a big deal. I mean, they're stuck with this for the rest of their lives. We had thrown around several names but could never settle on anything. We knew we wanted something that wasn't extremely common. On Friday, my school was having a fall festival where I had to work for a few hours that evening. To kill some time between school and the festival, I decided to get my nails done. Adam called me while I was in the chair, and I managed to answer with the hand she wasn't working on. He enthusiastically told me that he thought he knew what we should name our son. I didn't want the nail lady to start talking about me, so I told Adam to quickly tell me the name, then I had to go and we could talk about it later. He said he thought we should name him Isaiah. I said okay, hung up the phone, and didn't think much more about it. Just a few minutes later, my phone dinged that

I had received a random email from a church member. I glanced at my phone and saw the message, "FW: Isaiah 65:24." I was like, "Woah, this isn't a coincidence." The scripture says: "Before they call I will answer; while they are still speaking I will hear." I continued to read the rest of the story. It was written by a doctor who worked in Africa. It gave details of a young mother who had died in delivery, leaving behind a premature baby and a two-year-old daughter. The baby would need an incubator in order to live. In this remote area, they had no electricity and definitely no incubator. Only a hot water bottle would serve as a replacement for an incubator. Bottle after bottle they obtained burst. They kept going through struggle after struggle, trying to keep the baby alive. They were having a prayer time a few days later, and a ten-year-old girl prayed, "God, would send them a hot water bottle today to save the baby. Please send it today so this baby won't die. It will be no good tomorrow. And while You are about it, would You please send a dolly for the little girl so she'll know You really love her?"

Fast forward to the afternoon, the missionaries received word that they had a parcel. Inside were jerseys, bandages, boxes of raisins—and a brand-new hot water bottle. The leader rummaged down to the bottom of the box and found a beautifully dressed dolly. The ten-year-old asked if she could go with them to deliver the doll, and she did. What was amazing about this story was that this parcel would have been mailed five months before. God provided for this need in Africa. I knew He would provide for us as well. It sounded like, maybe, the name Isaiah was a perfect fit.

I didn't want to tell Adam about this over the phone. I went to work for a few hours at the fall festival then asked him to meet me for dinner. We had already talked about liking the name Isaiah, but we were looking for confirmation. I asked Adam why he felt this name was right. His devotional from this morning was from Adrian Rogers from the book of Isaiah titled, *When Delays Are a Blessing.* Rogers began with Isaiah 30:18: "And therefore will the Lord wait, that He may he gracious unto you." He also explained that, many times, the Lord will deliberately delay His graciousness to us. When Lazarus fell sick, his family sent for Jesus. Jesus didn't come immediately but waited because He had something greater in mind. God waited 4,000 years to send Jesus to us after He made His promise. God is never late, never early, never in a hurry. Rogers said, "Are you in a waiting game—praying days, weeks, months, even years for something—and God hasn't answered? Be still and know that in in the fullness of time, your request will be answered."

When Adam finished telling me about his devotion, I started tearing up and handed him my phone so he could see the title of the email I had gotten earlier after he called me. Then I had him read the rest of the story. He started tearing up as he was reading. Now we both looked crazy for crying in our booth at the Italian restaurant. There was no doubt that we had received confirmation that our child should be named Isaiah. We also looked up the meaning of this name. *Isaiah* means "the Lord helps me" or "salvation of God." The Lord has definitely helped us in the past, and He is truly our salvation. We got our son's name confirmed! Isaiah Stone. We chose Stone because God is not only our salvation, but He is also our rock.

C h a p t e r   1 3

The Isaiah Chapter

When we met Patricia and her parents, she asked if we would be okay with an open adoption. We never thought an open adoption could work. It's just weird. It's confusing. It's painful. How could that ever work? I can tell you how—God. Everything just felt right with Patricia and her parents. It didn't feel awkward. We just felt like extended family. Only God could make that happen. God had orchestrated this union years ago. Patricia had gone through the foster care system for years. Henry and Lee Ann started to foster her when she was nine and adopted her at age ten. Patricia told us that she knew the magnitude of her decision. She knew she was just a child and acknowledged that she couldn't give Isaiah everything she wanted. We were now going into this adoption with the goal of continuing a relationship with our birth mother and her family.

We began the frantic stage of preparing for parenthood. So much to buy. So much to do. So much to learn! We had already painted the nursery a gender-neutral color and bought bedding. Everything else was needed. The next month, Patricia would be going to the doctor, and she asked if we would like to get a 4D ultrasound done. I was ecstatic that we would get to see what Isaiah looked like. We were going to have the opportunity to experience some normal pregnancy things. We met Patricia and her mother at the ultrasound location. We went into a small room, and Patricia explained to the technician why Adam and I were in there. I got choked up again but managed to keep my tears at bay. I was so worried about her heart at that moment. She was getting to see pictures of her son for the first time.

Would this pull at her heartstrings so that she would want to keep him? I couldn't imagine carrying a child for nine months, feeling them move, seeing that precious face on the ultrasound, knowing that I would be giving that baby to someone else to raise. When I tell you that Patricia is wise beyond her years, it's the truth. I was in awe of her on this day, and that was just the beginning.

Our church and family members threw us baby showers. We had the nursery as ready as you could get. Plans were arranged for my maternity leave. I knew that my students would be in great hands because the lady doing my leave was the retiree, whose position I had filled. Now she will be filling mine for a few weeks. Isaiah was still comfortable in the womb, and he went past his due date. Patricia let us know that she would be induced on February 24 and to make plans to be there.

Adam and I packed our bags and Isaiah's bag and car seat in preparation for our trip to Scottsboro, where the delivery would take place. We got a hotel room because we would need to be at the hospital pretty early the next morning. It was so hard to sleep that night. Our lives were about to change forever in a matter of few hours. As we were preparing to go to the hospital that morning, I remember sitting on the bed and telling Adam, "We are about to be parents. Our lives will never be the same. This is our last day of just us." We prayed that everything would go smoothly and safely.

We got to the hospital around five in the morning. Patricia had already been induced, and they were hoping things would progress quickly. We stayed in the room with her for a little while, but we left because we could tell she was in pain. Her labor continued for several hours and went into the evening. Night had fallen, and she was still in active labor. We went back into the room again around ten-thirty and told her that we were going to stay in the waiting room. My mom, sister, and brother-in-law had come up to the hospital earlier that afternoon. Lanae and her husband, Joseph, left, but my mother stayed. It was beginning to storm outside, so we figured we should try and get some sleep. We had just closed our eyes around midnight when Lee Ann burst through the door and said, "If you're wanting to see this baby be delivered, you better come on!"

Oh wow! She was about to start pushing, and it was really getting real! We frantically walked to the room. I walked in past a curtain, then turned right back around. I had no clue what we were walking into. I turned to Adam and told him that he needed to keep his eyes on the window and that we would walk to her left side to be near her. I don't like medical stuff. Like those people that love to watch operations and others things like that? Yeah, that's not me. Adam sat down on a couch beside the bed, and I had to sit on his lap. I was seriously about to pass out. All I could think of was hoping and praying that Patricia would not look in my direction. I knew I had to be white as a ghost. She was in labor, about to birth a child that she's giving to *us*, and I was the one about to pass out. *Please don't look at me*, I kept thinking. Then she turned her head in my direction and asked if I was okay. I assured her that I was fine. Within the next few minutes, she delivered Isaiah at 12:45 a.m. He weighed in at nine pounds and five ounces. The doctors had no idea he would be that large. I looked over at him on the scale and turned back to Patricia smiling and said, "He's got your dimples!" I was really hoping he would inherit dimples. After they weighed him, the nurse asked Patricia where the baby should go. Patricia said, "Give him to his mother."

Goodness, I couldn't believe the words coming out of her mouth.

That was one of the most beautiful and painful moments in my entire lifetime. This strong and brave sixteen-year-old just went through almost twenty-four hours of labor and let me hold him first. My greatest joy came from someone's greatest pain. There are no words to describe that moment, except that it's a perfect picture of the gospel. God sent His Son for us. We don't deserve it, but He saw us worthy. Adam and I didn't deserve this baby, but Patricia saw past herself and selflessly decided, out of the deepest love, to give her child a future. We don't deserve Jesus, but God graciously gave us His Son to redeem and save us.

The next few hours were a whirlwind. They rolled Isaiah out in a crib, and we went back with the nurses to watch his first bath. Adam gave Isaiah his first bottle. We would eventually take Isaiah to our room, where my mom would meet her first grandchild. We took picture after picture. Around 3:00 a.m., a nurse came in and asked if we would want Isaiah to stay in the nursery so we could get a few hours of sleep. We agreed and squeezed into the hospital bed together. A nurse rolled Isaiah back into our room around 6:00 a.m.

Later that day, the nurse said that Patricia wanted to see the baby. They rolled him down to her room. Lee Ann texted me about a half hour later to ask for us to go to Patricia's room. We hugged Patricia as she was holding Isaiah. She was doing well physically after delivery. We bought her a Monster drink to celebrate because she loves those and hadn't been able to drink them while she was pregnant. We enjoyed our time together, and then it was time for Isaiah to go back for some of the normal newborn tests. We hugged again and went back to our room. Adam's parents and our sister-in-law came to meet Isaiah that afternoon. Brenda just cried and cried over our new blessing. She was still just in awe that someone would give us such a gift. A lot of tears were shed in our room.

On Sunday, we were released to go home. The agency caseworkers had encouraged Patricia to give Isaiah a gift. She made him a little blanket, and she gave him a dolphin snow globe that had been given to her by her birth mother. She had also written letters, one for me and one for Isaiah when he gets older. We all took pictures together, hugged, and cried before going home. I sat in the back seat while Adam drove. I cried for a good long while. Reality was setting in again. We were going home with a baby. Patricia was going home with thoughts of her sacrifice. We felt so unworthy of this blessed gift. I prayed over Patricia during our drive. I prayed that God would give her strength, comfort, and a quick healing of her body.

With adoption, states have varying laws regarding the time line of relinquishing rights. Patricia signed papers in the hospital, but she still had the option to change her mind within a certain time frame. It was hard not to think about this, but I couldn't let it consume me. God had worked everything out so far, so I tried to remember that He wouldn't fail me now.

We settled into parenthood fairly quickly. Lots of people wanted to come by to visit to see our new blessing. My mom and Brenda loved to dote over him. Everyone at church was thrilled over having a new baby in our church, and they were so happy for Adam and me. Shortly after we got home, I sat on our bed to read the letter Patricia had written to me. I squalled and squalled. She wrote about how she knew she was giving Isaiah a better life and how she had prayed for the perfect parents to raise him. I was just in awe of her words. I'm glad now that I didn't read this letter at the hospital because I was an emotional wreck after it. We were blessed so much by her.

Before Isaiah was two months old, I was home alone with him on a Saturday near Easter. I began watching *The Passion of the Christ*. I had seen this film several times, but it was my first time watching it as a mother. As Mary was watching her son carry our cross in excruciating pain, I lost it. I could not even fathom seeing my Isaiah going through that. Moms are supposed to fix things. I was sure her initial instinct was to try to save her son. I was holding my sleeping child while I squalled. I was ugly-crying, splotchy-face crying.

But I realized God had prepared Mary for that agonizing time. He had already prepared her while carrying Jesus as a virgin. The ridicule she must have endured—and now she had to watch her son suffer. What faith Mary had, fully trusting in her God. I realized that only faith in a God, who would provide, got her through.

After a few months, Isaiah's adoption was set to be finalized. We had met with our caseworker and attorney to go over what to expect on our Gotcha Day. Our caseworker, Renee, had previously heard about my shooting during our home study. She shared this information with the attorney. This lady had tears in her eyes and said, "Oh my goodness! I saw you on the news, and I prayed for you! I can't believe you are here, and I'm so thankful you are okay!"

I told her that God had taken care of me throughout that ordeal and He had made good from it. We all went into the judge's chambers to finalize our adoption. The attorney shared my story, briefly, with the judge through teary eyes. This judge was visibly taken aback by my story. He told me, "I am so sorry that this happened to you. Young lady, I know exactly why God spared you. He saved you so that you could be this little boy's momma. How could I not approve this adoption?"

Isaiah officially became a Rogers on May 17, 2011. A neat part of this story was that Patricia's birthday was the day before. What's more, my best friend and her husband were celebrating the birth of their adoptive child on this same day! Our adoption was finalized as theirs was just beginning. Only God could weave a story together like that.

Exactly three months later, my sister gave birth to my new nephew! My mom, Isaiah, and I headed to the hospital to await his arrival. We got word that she was going to need an emergency C-section. After we knew about his delivery and weight, my mom asked me if I wanted to call Dad to tell him about the baby. I said no, and I had no idea that I would regret this decision for the rest of my life. Just two days later, I would be called to the office at school. I was scared to death because they told me to bring my stuff. I was praying the entire time I was walking to the office, thinking something had happened to Adam or Isaiah. I walked into my principal's office to see Adam sitting in a chair. Whew. He was okay. Isaiah must be okay because Adam seemed fine. Adam had to deliver the devastating news that my dad had been found dead that morning. He was gone.

The next few hours were a complete blur. My dad was no longer here. He died alone on his recliner. He never even got to meet his second grandchild in person. Even though he spent a lot of his life making poor choices, he was still my dad. A huge piece of my life was gone now. And I should've talked to him two days before, but no, I had been selfish and ignored him. I still struggle with that decision to this day. It was a whirlwind, trying to plan a funeral for your parent. My dad had always coached my sister and me in softball. All the team girls loved him. I enjoyed making a softball display of pictures in his honor. Several of his former players came to express their condolences. The softball-loving, goofy, early-church-service-going Dad was the one I wanted to remember.

We were so blessed to have Isaiah during this time of tragedy. Having this baby gave us joy in the midst of great sorrow. That was another confirmation that God is never late, never early, but always right on time. He gave us this baby at the exact time we would need him.

Chapter 14

Change Is Coming, and It's Hard

July 20, 2012, would be another day that stopped me in my tracks. That was the day of the mass shooting at a movie theater in Aurora, Colorado. I was again paralyzed with fear. I had been doing so well with my mental recovery, but I was now riveted to everything on the television. How could someone be so cruel? Those people were just trying to enjoy a movie. We go to movies all the time, and now, I was planning to check all my surroundings next time we went. My heart was breaking for those who lost loved ones. I also hurt for those that survived this horrid attack because now they would be dealing with a similar emotional trauma as I did. My experience allowed me to pray specifics over those that he had hurt—both physically and mentally.

The following year was pretty calm, except for a scare that we had with Isaiah. One day, I got a call from his preschool about him having a pretty high temperature. I talked to my principal and asked if I could leave to take Isaiah to the doctor. I picked him up and was only a few minutes away from his school when he stopped talking to me. I looked in my rearview mirror to find him drooling and his body twitching. I quickly pulled over into a store parking lot, called my sister-in-law, who had him at the preschool, and asked her to come fast. He was having a seizure, and I didn't know what to do. Adam was too far away to help right then. She was with us within a matter of minutes. I called 911, and she got in the back with Isaiah while I drove. I couldn't watch. We met an ambulance several miles down the road. Adam left work immediately to meet us as well. We headed to Children's of Alabama hospital. Isaiah was always very talkative, and he wasn't saying anything. I was scared to death. I kept asking the EMT if his behavior was normal after a seizure, and they assured me that it was.

About halfway to Birmingham, Isaiah started talking more. My heart was so relieved to see some semblance of normalcy out of him. They ran several tests on him and determined that he had, had a febrile seizure, which was caused by a sudden spike in temperature. We were told to monitor him in the future when he got a temperature. Doctors explained that he should grow out of this by the time he was two or three. He had two more febrile seizures within the next year or so but hasn't had a single seizure since then.

Shortly after Isaiah turned two, we started the adoption process again. We were building a house, so we decided to wait until we moved so we wouldn't have to do two home studies. Lifeline Children's Services helped finalize our adoption with Isaiah, so we decided to go with this agency for our second child. We were so excited to be working with Renee again. Our first home visit was conducted in October 2013. Two more home visits were done in November then in early April 2014. I had been working on our profile book months before we started the adoption process. I knew I could get that completed early in hopes of speeding things up. Our home study was finally complete and approved on July 10, 2014. Now we were just playing the waiting game for another round. This time was a little bit easier, initially because we had Isaiah as our reminder of God's faithfulness. He provided for us once, so we had faith that He would do it again.

We went through the rest of 2014 with very few prospects. The entire year of 2015 would be the same. After we went an entire year with few leads on a match, Adam and I prayed about joining a second agency that was nationwide. My best friend, Ceje, had used AdoptHelp based in California when they adopted Zoe. I looked up their website and felt very encouraged because the majority of families were matched with a birth mother in less than a year. I was so excited by that! Adam and I both agreed to go ahead with a second agency to increase our chances of getting a baby. I emailed a caseworker with our information for us to get the process started.

I got an informational packet in the mail from AdoptHelp at the beginning of June. I started filling out pages upon pages of paperwork. Just a few weeks later, we received an email from the Lifeline caseworker, Renee, about a young birth mother named Gabrielle. With Lifeline, they would send us birth mother information, and we would be able to decide whether or not to have our profile shown. I was thrilled over this possibility, but now we were unsure about what to do with AdoptHelp. Do we hold off or continue? Well, our decision was made for us. Gabrielle chose another adoptive family. We again felt the roller coaster of emotions. Another rejection.

We did continue with AdoptHelp and had everything completed and ready to go around mid-September. With this agency, we had to get a different profile book created. We used a lady the agency recommended, who makes profile books for a living. This entire design process was $750. Then we would have to purchase books on top of that cost. The agency suggested starting with forty-to fifty profile books initially. This would cost us around $500. They would send our profile book out to any birth mother that matched our filters. We would be updated monthly on how many birth mothers had viewed our profile.

On the same day that we were officially approved with AdoptHelp, I got an email from a friend about learning to wait on God—the hardest part. If we are honest, I don't think any of us enjoy waiting. We are always in a hurry, but this wait was different. It's so hard when you have a yearning and desire that isn't being fulfilled. Waiting may be the hardest single thing we are called to do. It's frustrating, but we can turn to the Bible and see that God often told people to wait. The Bible is full of accounts of His faithfulness and His purpose in the wait. I can't imagine being the Israelites. God told them they wouldn't be enslaved in Egypt forever and would become a new nation, but they had to wait 400 years for that to happen! Or when they had to wait forty years in the wilderness before making it to the Promised Land. I highly doubt I would've stayed encouraged or positive during that time. The email included a quote from Ben Patterson: "The work that God does within us while we wait is just as important as whatever it is we are waiting for." This was the exact, timely encouragement I needed during our wait.

Around this same time, Patricia's mother, Lee Ann, was very sick. She was no longer able to work. Her health was fading fast. She ended up passing away in January 2016. My senior Sunday school teacher, Bonnie, also lost her battle with cancer at the same time. Their funeral services were on the same day. I called my mom and told her that I really felt like we needed to be there for Patricia and Henry. I asked her to give my love and prayers to the Moore family for me. Adam, his parents, Isaiah, and I headed to Scottsboro to the funeral home.

I had no clue of the amazing things that would occur while we were there. We saw Henry almost immediately as we walked in. We hugged him and told him how sorry we were over his loss. As we continued down the aisle, we were stopped by person after person. These were family members of Lee Ann and Henry. They were so happy to meet us and felt as though they really knew us because of our relationship with Patricia. We made it down the aisle to where Patricia was standing near her mother's casket. We hugged and cried. Isaiah hugged her and continued standing next to her for the remainder of our time there. I asked him later if he wanted to move and go sit down. He just said, "Nope. I want to stay here with Patricia." Patricia later said that Isaiah staying with her was like a balm to those hurting over Lee Ann, because family and friends were meeting him for the first time, just as SHE had been a similar balm as when she was adopted. Lee Ann's mother or something died, and friends and family were getting to meet Patricia for the first time. Full circle— soothed hearts.

I walked back to my seat with a huge lump in my throat. God had given this little four-year-old a huge, compassionate heart. We asked him later that night why he wanted to stand with her for so long. He said, "I just felt like I needed to be there with her."

Sheesh. Another lump in the throat and more tears. He was not quite five, but he had the wherewithal to care for others in time of need. We also got to meet Patricia's foster family that cared for her for several years. The entire night was another example of what God *can* do. We thought an open adoption would never work, but there we are at a funeral where it felt like family. Nothing was awkward. (And a sidenote: we had met with Patricia and her family every year since Isaiah's birth and continue to do so to this day. Henry sends Isaiah money for Christmas and his birthday.) Only God could've orchestrated this union that would turn into family.

As more time passed without a match, we had to pay for an updated home study and home visit. By March 2016, we only had three profile books left. This was encouraging and depressing at the same time. This meant that thirty-seven different birth mothers had viewed our profile book since the beginning of October. It was discouraging because that meant thirty-seven rejections and the need to purchase more books. With this agency, they did a lot of advertising on Google. That's how so many families were matched quickly. We also had to make payment installments for these advertising services. I'm only sharing this money information to help explain the financial strains that come with adoption. Adam has always been smart financially, so I knew we would be okay through this adoption process and adding a second agency. With our first adoption, we had done a few fundraisers to help cover the adoption costs. We started saving money early on for our second adoption, but going with two agencies increased our cost. We ended up taking out a line of credit on our home to help cover expenses.

On March 15, I ordered more profile books. I was a little depressed because so many people had viewed our books, and yet, we weren't picked. It was like a bazillion times worse than being picked last for a team in gym class. I ordered forty more book that cost us $492. I was grumbling to myself that it seems like we just keep spending more and more money. Later that evening, Adam told me that he had gotten a call earlier from a family friend. This person had lost a loved one a few months ago and wanted to give Isaiah some money to go toward his college fund. The amount? $500. My jaw dropped because I knew God used that to speak directly to me. He was reminding me to quit worrying about the finances behind adoption. Quit worrying about the wait. Quit trying to fix things. He is in control. He's got his. I just need to rest in Him. I mean, what are the odds that I just spent nearly $500 and then find out my child is given that amount in the same day? That's just how God works. Always on time. Never early. Never late. It was exactly the reminder I needed. I needed to be reminded that He is always at work, even if I can't see it or feel it.

Throughout the year, my granddaddy's health had gone downhill. He had a lung plication surgery back in 2010, and his health just continued to decline from there. He was always a get-up-and-go person. He helped me move every time I would change apartments in college. He loved to travel. We took several trips with them as we got older. He loved to serve others. He drove the church bus for almost forty years! He and Grandma would go with us to every court session. To see his mobility so limited was heartbreaking. He had vascular dementia, COPD, and congestive heart failure. We visited them more often because we weren't really sure how much time he would have left. During one of our visits a year before, Granddaddy was sitting in a recliner. He wasn't really talking much and would fall asleep in the chair. Isaiah got up from playing, walked over to Granddaddy, and put his little arms around his neck and just hugged him. Didn't say a word. Isaiah just closed his eyes and held my granddaddy close. It was such a precious moment that I'm thankful to have caught on camera. My grandma was unable to provide all the help he needed, so they had caregivers there daily. I remember the last time I saw him. He was in a hospital bed in their bedroom. I leaned over his bedside and told him how much I loved him, how proud I was to be his granddaughter, and how I had been so blessed with incredible grandparents. I said to him, "Granddaddy, if you see Jesus calling you home, you need to go. We're going to miss you, but we are okay. You can go home."

I kissed him on the cheek, unaware if he even knew what I was saying to him. But I was so thankful to have had that moment with him because I didn't get that with my paw-paw or dad. My granddaddy went to be with the Lord on April 29. Isaiah sang a verse or two of "Lord, I Lift Your Name on High" at Granddaddy's funeral. His service was one of the most beautiful I've ever attended. It was a celebration service of a life well lived. And I have no doubt that he's singing tenor in the heavenly choir.

By June, we were out of profiles again. I ordered forty more books—more money again, another roller coaster of emotions from this. We got an update from Lifeline in July that they had very few prospects of new birth mothers. On July 15, we heard from Kathryn at AdoptHelp that we were a birth mother's second choice. Ugh. Second choice. I guess that's better than not being chosen at all. Trying to look on the bright side. Trying.

On July 3, I had tucked Isaiah into bed, and we said our prayers together. When we finished, Isaiah said that he was so glad that Patricia gave him to me. I told him that I was happy as well. I explained that she loved him so much to be able to do that. She made a hard decision, but she did it because of how much she loved him. He paused for a minute and said, "I think she did it because of what it would mean for you. Now you've got a baby."

I couldn't help but cry. How on earth could my five-year-old understand things so deeply? This also made me cry more because I knew that Isaiah would make such a great brother. He prayed every night that God would give him a baby brother or sister. We've always been up front with Isaiah about adoption. He has always known how special he was and how much of a gift he was to everyone around us. My children will always know about the love and sacrifice that comes with adoption. I went to bed weepy that night and asking that God would answer our prayers soon.

On August 16, Adam and I got an email from a caseworker named Mia at AdoptHelp. A birth mother had chosen us! I couldn't believe it. We hadn't even been with them for a year, and we were matched! My heart was racing. Mia wanted to email us about the birth mother's situation to see if it is something we were open to. Her name was Kim, and she was due on our around January 12, gender unknown. She was homeless and living from hotel to hotel. The birth father was aware of the pregnancy, but he was in jail. Kim believed he would sign any documents needed in adoption. She was thirty-five and had four other children that did not currently live with her. Her youngest was in foster care. Her oldest was eighteen and no longer living with her. She had lived a rough, dysfunctional life but was trying to get it back together. She believed adoption was the best plan for her child because she knew she wanted the best life for her baby—not one that would go into state care. She had state-funded medical insurance, but she wasn't going to the doctor regularly for prenatal visits.

If we wanted to go forward with this adoption, we would be responsible for her financially from this point and until six to eight weeks after birth and placement. That meant $550 for housing, $400 for food, $60 for cell phone, and $150 for transportation each month. This was August. She was not due until January. We were looking at six months or more of expenses. Could we even swing that financially? That was not even including the adoption expenses for the agency! So we were looking at spending around $7,000 just to provide aid to the birth mother. What happened if we did all this and she changed her mind in the hospital? We would be out thousands of dollars. But then again—who says no to a possible baby? Adam and I discussed various scenarios and made the decision a matter of prayer. We asked our closest friends and family members to pray for guidance along with us.

After lots of prayer, neither of us felt at peace with this baby situation. I prayed so hard for God to make this decision crystal clear. I am the queen of second-guessing and overanalyzing. I did not want to spend the next few months agonizing over this decision and wondering if we had done the wrong thing. I was reminded of Matthew 5:37 that says, "Simply let your 'Yes' be 'Yes' and your 'No' 'No.' Anything more than these comes from evil." God is not the author of confusion, so I clung to the fact that any doubtful thoughts were not from Him. Adam and I contacted the agency and told them that we didn't have a peace about this situation and would have to say no.

As the weeks and months continued to roll on without a match, those negative thoughts started creeping back into my mind. Did we make the right decision? Did we just say no because of the money situation? I prayed that God would once again speak peace unto my heart. I knew we made the right decision. Those damaging thoughts needed to flee. God had always been faithful to me, and I knew He wouldn't stop now. When I would see other people with babies or women, who were pregnant, my jealousy and insecurities would creep back in. But being covetous means that we are discontent with what God has blessed us with already. Adam and I had already been blessed far more than we deserved, so I needed to cling to that.

November rolled around, and we were running low on profile books yet again and needed to order more. We celebrated Thanksgiving and Christmas with friends and family. The year 2016 ended without a baby.

God Shows Off Again

It was now 2017. Isaiah was about to turn six. Sheesh. I really didn't want my children to have so many years between them. I mean, we started this adoption process when Isaiah was two and a half! I obviously couldn't change the age gap, so I was just going to have to keep trusting. The next few months continued to roll on without a match. Our home study had expired yet again, so we were having to schedule an updated visit. More money gone. More frustration from year after year of nothing.

My maw-maw (my dad's mother) had been in an assisted living facility for a few years. She had been doing well until we got news that she had pancreatic cancer. She went downhill extremely fast. The cancer was very aggressive, and my maw-maw passed away less than two weeks later. Now she was reunited with her husband and her son. When I tell you that I am truly blessed by my grandparents, it's the truth. I could not have asked for better grandparents.

Adam and I were at the point where we were wondering if God didn't want us to have any more children. We prayed for God to reveal this to us. He and I both agreed that this would be our last year of pursuing adoption. We would not renew our home study after it expired next time. If we didn't have a child by the end of this year, it was over.

My heart was breaking again. God knew the desires of my heart. He knew how badly I wanted another child. He knew how much Isaiah wanted a brother or sister. But I knew that His ways are higher than ours. Surrendering my plans was extremely painful, but I knew it was the right thing to do. With tear-filled eyes, I prayed for God's will to be done and not mine.

Another big change this year involved my job. My school system was reconfiguring. Our separate elementary schools were merging into feeder schools of each other. No longer would each school house grades K-5. My current school was going to have second and third grades, so I had to pack up my entire classroom to move buildings. I was moving to a building, which would become an intermediate school for grades four to six. I wasn't really happy with the move. No one seemed to be, really, but we had no choice. I was determined to make the best of this move and the new adventure that awaited us. All my classroom boxes and belongings were put on a moving truck and sent to Maddox. I would set up my classroom later that summer.

Now Isaiah and I were going to get to spend some fun time together! We love going to the movies together, and he had been wanting to go watch *The Boss Baby*. I looked around at some theaters near us, and Decatur was the only place still showing the movie. I called Mom and asked if we could come spend the night after the movie. She was happy to have us, so I packed up our stuff and headed for Decatur.

Isaiah and I got settled in the theater before the movie started. There may have only been fifteen people in the theater for this matinee. The movie starts out with the main character, Tim, explaining how his family is perfect. He's a seven-year-old (close to Isaiah's age). The mother has red hair. The father is wearing glasses. It's just the three of them. It's so very similar to my own family. Tim proceeds to say that he loves the way his family is right now because three is the perfect number. He compared his family to a triangle and how that shape is the strongest found in nature.

I had the biggest lump in my throat and was fighting back tears. This was a children's movie, and I was already crying within the first five minutes. Was this movie God's sign to me that we were just supposed to be a family of three? Are we just supposed to be the strongest force with just three of us? I've always had a fascination with numbers and their significance, so was God using this just for me? I pushed back the tears and prayed in the theater quietly. I pleaded with God for Him to just open a door or shut it. I was okay either way. *Please just shut the door or open it. Make it so evident that no doubts will ever creep in. Just open the door or shut it.*

We continued watching the movie. Tim's family ended up getting a new baby in their house. This Boss Baby behaves normally around the adults, but he acts/talks like an adult when they aren't looking. Tim becomes increasingly jealous of the baby because he requires so much attention from his parents. Long story short, these two never get along. Both of them end up getting grounded until they can learn to get along. Without spoiling too many details of the movie, the Boss Baby is going to be taken back to Baby Corp (where he originally came from), and Tim's family would not remember the baby being there at all. However, Tim and Baby end up realizing how much they truly do love each other and would miss each other. Tim invites Baby back to his family. Their perfect triangle of love turns into a heart—with enough love for each another. Now they are a perfect heart.

Mercy, there I was crying in the theater again! I wanted the heart of love, not the triangle. Isaiah's been praying specifically for a little brother, just like what happened in this movie. I wiped away the tears again and prayed as we left the theater.

Not long after leaving, Isaiah and I were getting hungry. We decided to swing by the drive-through at Krystal's before heading to Mom's house. I had just placed our order and pulled forward when I got a phone call from an unknown number. I normally don't answer those, but I did that time. It was our caseworker from California, and she asked if it was a good time to talk. I told her that I was in line to pay for food and that she was on speaker phone through my car. She waited for me to pay for our food then I pulled forward to stop to talk. She told me that a birth mother had chosen us! I was in complete and utter shock. My entire body was trembling, and my heart was racing. Was this for real?

She told me that the birth mother was named Courtney and that we were the *only* family she was interested in. She was due in August. (I was so excited, but my heart sank. August, really? I'm a teacher. That's a horrible timing at the start of the year. I pushed that aside and kept listening.) Courtney saw my red hair in our profile picture from the AdoptHelp website and immediately clicked to view our profile. She has red hair too! That's why I caught her eye initially. She read through our profile and liked everything she read about us. I was about to take a bite of my burger when the caseworker told me that Courtney worked at a Krystal's. Say what? This was no coincidence. (Decatur has tons of fast-food restaurants. What were the odds of me getting a call about a birth mother while I was eating at the same franchise that employs her?) Then she told me that Courtney lives in Scottsboro. Again, my jaw is dropped. I could not believe what I was hearing. Red hair, Krsytal's, and she also lives in the same city where Isaiah was born? Are you kidding me? This agency is in California. Only God could match us up all the way from California to a birth mother in *our* state and in the exact same city as our previous birth mother. And it got better—the caseworker said Courtney has two boys, one of which is named Izaiah. *Are you kidding me?* I was seriously at a loss for words. I had to catch my breath in order for me to tell the caseworker of all these similarities. I was completely blown away. There was no doubt in my mind that this was a God-thing. I asked for Him to move, and He did in a mighty way. This was definitely a door opening—loud and clear. And guess what else? She was having a boy. Isaiah had been praying specifically for a baby brother.

Now I had a problem. I couldn't stay at my mom's house after all. I had to get home to tell Adam this news in person. I did not want to do it over the phone. But I had arrived in my mom's driveway. Should I tell her now or just make up some excuse as to why we couldn't spend the night? Do I just leave and call her on my way home? I decided to call Ceje, my friend, who was serving as local lawyer liaison, first to ask her what I was supposed to do regarding the agency. This was totally different than when we adopted Isaiah. Ceje told me that the birth mother had picked us and we didn't really have to do anything else except say yes or no. The rest was just waiting until the birth. I told her that she was the first person to know about us possibly getting a baby. She was thrilled for us and said she would be praying for me as I tried to figure out what to do.

Isaiah was in the car with me during this entire conversation with our caseworker. I had turned off the car speaker shortly after we started talking. But Isaiah still heard enough. I unbuckled my seat belt and turned toward him in the back. I asked him how much of the conversation he heard. He said he heard something about a birth mother and that she was having a boy. I told him that he was right, and I asked him what he thought about having a baby brother. He had the sweetest giggle and said he would really like that. After seeing Isaiah's joy, I decided that I would let him tell his Nonnie and pops that he was going to get a baby brother. We left all our bags in the car and walked to the front door. He just kept giggling and saying that he couldn't believe that he was actually going to get a brother!

I'm glad that I got my phone out quickly to record Isaiah because he ran straight into the house and shared the news. My mom was sitting in the exact same chair as when we told her about Isaiah. My mom was in total shock. She was smiling, crying, and hugging Isaiah. She said, "How long have you known?"

I laughed and told her only about fifteen minutes! I filled my mother in on all the details. She was amazed. Then we put our heads together to figure out a creative way for us to tell Adam the big news. My mom has always been extremely crafty, and she was preparing to teach a craft class in a week. She had already planned on Isaiah being her guinea pig so she could have an example to take with her. It was a craft for Father's Day. This is perfect! She had men's gardening gloves, and each child would put their handprints on the gloves. She suggested we do one hand for Isaiah and the other would be blank except for August 2017. We got it finished, and it turned out great! I had another problem though—how was I going to tell Adam that we were coming back home? I'm a terrible liar. I started out with just texting him, instead of calling. Like I said, I'm a bad liar. At least texting would give me some time to come up with an excuse. I told him that I wasn't feeling well and wanted to come home. He was pretty insistent for me to stay, saying that Mom could take care of Isaiah while I rested. Shoot. I knew this wouldn't work. Then I decided to tell him that Pops, my mom's husband, Mike, was talking nonstop and was getting on my nerves. (Sorry, Mike! I love you so much!)

Adam reluctantly agreed and told me to be careful coming home. I could tell he still thought I should've stayed at Mom's house.

We hugged Mom and Mike goodbye and headed out. Mom had to keep all this quiet because no one else knew yet! But it was such an exciting secret! Isaiah and I had an hour's drive to get home. He began asking me different questions about his future baby brother. I explained as much as I could to him. We also talked about how he would present the gloves to his Daddy-O and tell him that he's getting a baby brother.

We made it back to the house, and I got my camera ready. Isaiah didn't waste any time again! Adam was sitting on the recliner, watching TV. Isaiah walked over to the arm of the chair. He said, "This glove is my hand, and this other one is for my baby brother."

Adam looked puzzled and said, "What?"

Isaiah repeated that he was going to be getting a baby brother. Adam then looked at me and asked if this was for real. I told him yes. We are getting a baby! He asked when, and I told him to look at the glove because it said, "August." He still looked dumbfounded and asked again if this was for real and how?! Isaiah just giggled and smiled the entire time. I stopped recording at this point because my voice was getting choked up. I sat down on the couch to explain all the details to Adam.

We then discussed how and when we would tell the rest of our family. We were going to wait a little bit before telling our church family or announcing anything on social media. We knew, with adoption, that things could change in an instant, so we wanted to keep our circle fairly small, so we only told our closest friends and family members. I was corresponding back and forth with our caseworker about Courtney. She gave us Courtney's phone number for us to be able to talk with her. I began texting Courtney shortly after I got her number, and we set up a time to talk on the phone with Adam. We hit off after just a few minutes of conversation with her. It didn't feel forced or awkward. We shared with her all the examples of how God orchestrated the meeting of our families. She couldn't believe it and was in amazement, just like the rest of us. She and I would continue to text back and forth from this point forward.

After a few weeks, we decided it was a good time to tell our church family our exciting news. Since Adam was our music minister, it wasn't uncommon for Isaiah to come up on the stage with him. We all stood on the stage after the service was over. Adam told the congregation that Isaiah had some news to share. He got the microphone and said, "Hey! Did you know I'm getting a baby brother?"

That moment was so sweet and one I will never forget. Our church family was cheering and clapping and crying. They had been praying along with us for so long, so they were joyous to see an answered prayer.

It was going to be a very busy summer from this point on! I already knew it was going to be crazy because I was having to change schools and completely set up a new classroom. Now we had to get the nursery set up as well. My mom also asked me where she was going to sleep since the extra bedroom would now be a nursery. When we built our house, we had a bonus room started above our garage. We had the walls covered with wallboard and primed, but that was it. We needed to get this bonus room finished so my mom could have a place to sleep after the baby is born. We picked out a color we both agreed on, and I got the entire bonus room painted. In the summer, without air-conditioning—phew. We picked out carpet and scheduled a time for insulation. Those poor fellows were sweating so badly. I kept offering them extra water or tea because it was so hot. I could at least paint in the early morning when it was cooler, but they didn't have that luxury. We did some research on freestanding AC/heat units to install upstairs. By the end of the summer, we had the bonus room almost complete. We also got my classroom set up and finished, thanks to help from some friends and family.

We also tried to decide on a name during this time. Like with Isaiah, we had tossed around a few names here and there. We knew we wanted another biblical name, preferably Old Testament. We liked the name Malachi and would call him Chi. But then I didn't like that name because I was afraid people would pronounce his name Chi as in the Greek pronunciation. I knew I wanted the name William somewhere. William was my granddaddy's first name. Adam and I finally agreed on the name Gideon. I had always liked his story in the Bible. He trusted God, even when things were scary. He was a mighty warrior of God. Who wouldn't want their child to be named after that? (I was also a fan of the TV series *Criminal Minds*, and Jason Gideon was my favorite character!) So we decided our new addition would be named Gideon William. Our church had a baby shower for us in July. One of my friends painted a tree on canvas, and guests added their thumbprints and names along branches. Gideon's full name was also written there. This was how Grandma found out that we would be naming our child after her sweet husband. We got the nursery complete shortly after the shower, and now we were just waiting for him to get here!

Chapter 16

The Gideon Chapter

My official first day back at school was August 7. The first day of school was August 15. Gideon's due date: August 22. This schedule would maybe give me a week with my students before I had to leave. My new principal had been made aware of our adoption earlier in the summer, and we already had a substitute lined up for my maternity leave. She was on standby in case the baby decided to come earlier. I made it through a week of professional development, orientation, and a full week with my students! Courtney was going to be induced on the twenty-second, so I decided that Friday the eighteenth would be my last day. I wanted to have Monday to get some last-minute things completed before we headed to Chattanooga for the birth.

On Sunday morning, Adam left for church around eight. I was getting ready for church around nine when I got a text from Courtney that she was in labor. Oh boy. It was going to take us at least three hours to get to Chattanooga. I had to call Adam fast. I knew he probably wouldn't answer his phone, so I called his brother, Brad, who usually got to church early. I told him the news, and he said he would pass this along to Adam. He would also talk to his wife about coming to get Isaiah since he wouldn't be going with us to the hospital. I was in a rush before Adam got home. I already had a bag packed for the baby, but we had nothing packed for us! I was planning on getting all that done the next day! I was frantically packing for myself and getting a few necessities for Adam to help him out before he got home.

Once Adam arrived, he finished his packing. Brad's wife, Stephanie, came by to get Isaiah to take him to church with her.

Just a few minutes before she got there, we were rushing around in the bathroom and knocked off a bottle of nail polish. It shattered on our tile floor and into the grout. We were panicking and trying to figure out how to get this cleaned up quickly so we could leave! It wasn't hard to get the polish off the tile, but it was almost impossible to clean out of the grout. It just kept spreading every time we tried to clean it. When Stephanie arrived, she told us to go. She and her girls would try to clean it up as best as they could. We finally left the house around ten. (And for the record, we still have a little pink polish in our grout to this day!)

Another snag in our trip was that we needed to gas up the car. That had also been on my list to get completed on Monday! We planned to stop around Scottsboro. We found a gas station that had a Wendy's right next door. Adam filled up the car while I ran over to get us some lunch. We had no idea what would happen in the hospital, so we knew it was important to go ahead and eat. During the drive, I was calling or texting friends and family to let them know what was going on and to be praying. I was so worried about missing something. We were fortunate to be in the delivery room with Isaiah, and I was really wanting the same experience with Gideon. But it was also going to be strange as it would be our first time to meet Courtney in person. I was planning on us meeting her in the hospital before she was induced. Well, that was not happening now! I prayed that everything would go smoothly and that we would get there in time to not miss anything. Our hearts were racing because everything was happening so suddenly, and we were headed to a hospital completely unknown to us!

We made it to the hospital around 2:00 p.m., found a place to park, left all our bags in the car, and started to navigate our way around the hospital. We found the information desk that directed us toward labor and delivery. We made it to that floor and explained to a nurse at the desk who we were and why we were there. They gave us visitor passes to wear and directed us to a room to wait. After about ten to fifteen minutes, a doctor came in to tell us that Gideon had already been born. He said that everything had gone well and that he and Courtney were doing fine. I asked about how much he weighed, and the doctor guessed around six or seven pounds. He told us that someone would be with us shortly for us to get to see the baby.

I thought I would be devastated to have missed the birth, but I honestly wasn't. I just had an overwhelming peace. He was okay. Courtney was okay. It was all going to be fine. That was just another God-thing where He gives you peace. I never once felt upset or sad about missing the delivery. We also found out that he was born at the exact time we were walking in the hospital—2:00 p.m. on the dot.

We were texting and calling family and friends to let them know that Gideon was here and doing well. Ten minutes have passed, and we were still sitting in the room with no news. Then thirty minutes. Forty minutes.

At this point, I was starting to get concerned. *Did something happen to Gideon? Is Courtney okay? Is she changing her mind?* Our minds were spinning and trying not to be overwhelmed with worry. I called our lawyer liaison and friend Ceje to see if she knew anything because I was really getting nervous. She told me that she'll get back with us. Ceje called the hospital to ask for an update. The nurse that was supposed to be coming to get us called Ceje back. The nurse felt it would be better for Ceje to talk to us about an update instead of a nurse. Ceje called us back after an excruciating hour of waiting. She assured us that everything was fine with Gideon and Courtney, but she did have some unexpected news. He was biracial. Courtney was so worried that we would think she lied to us or that we wouldn't want him anymore. Of course we wanted him! It never crossed our minds not to want him! Yes, we wanted him! Were we surprised a lit-tle by this news? Sure. But we knew that God was all over this. There was no doubt in my mind that this child was supposed to be ours.

Ceje called the nurse back to tell her that we still wanted to pursue this adoption and couldn't wait to meet him! Around three-twenty, we were finally able to meet our newest addition!

I wish I could tell you that I had a love-at-first-sight moment, but I didn't. I didn't have that with Isaiah either. I think it was more of a me problem than anything because I honestly don't think babies are beautiful when they are so fresh. Everything is so squished and puffy. Poor Isaiah had a ridge on his head, but he had the most adorable chubby cheeks. Hehe. Gideon also had sweet cheeks and a headful of hair. Unruly hair! And guess what else he had? Dimples! I researched this later and found out that only around 20 to 30 percent of the population has dimples. We were going to have two children with dimples! Only God could do that. We got to keep Gideon in our room with us while we were in the hospital. I had bought a small gift to give to Courtney. I wanted something that had meaning. I found a sweet little necklace that had two intertwined hearts on it. I explained on a card the symbolism of hearts. It represented that our hearts would forever be connected because of Gideon and that he would always know how much he is loved by her.

The next day, my mom came to the hospital with Isaiah and my grandmother. Our friend Joy had made a matching shirt and onesie for the new brothers. Isaiah was thrilled to get to meet his baby brother for the first time. We had him sit on the bed with Gideon on his lap. He just giggled and talked about how cute he was. He was fascinated by his little fingers and toes. We took pictures after pictures of the sweet brothers together. My mom and grandmother were also overjoyed to meet our newest blessing. Ceje and her aunt also made it to the hospital in order for her to take care of some of her legal obligations for AdoptHelp. Ceje met with Courtney about the adoption process, and she signed the needed paperwork to continue with the adoption plan.

August 21 was also the day of the total solar eclipse. Mom and I decided to take Isaiah downstairs to view the eclipse. Thankfully, Ceje and her aunt had eclipse glasses, and they preferred to love on the baby instead of seeing the eclipse. They loaned us their glasses, and we headed downstairs. You could tell it was getting closer to the total eclipse because people were piling outside. We were just looking up through some skylights in the hospital when I spotted Courtney and her mother. My mom had never seen her before. I hadn't seen her in person either! We stopped to talk. I hugged her, and I introduced my mother and Isaiah. She was wearing the necklace we had given her, and she told me how much she loved it. My mom looked at Courtney and told her that she wasn't sure how to even say thank-you to her. We were all starting to get teary-eyed, so we hugged again and went to view the eclipse with Isaiah.

Later that afternoon, Courtney asked if she could see Gideon. We put him in his little cradle and rolled him down to her room. She and her mother wanted some time with him. Adam and I decided to go eat dinner with Mom, Grandmother, and Isaiah while he was out of our room. (It was a nice distraction for me.) We walked downstairs and found a sandwich place within walking distance of the hospital. Courtney texted me shortly after we had finished eating and told me that we could come back to get Gideon. We brought Isaiah with us to Courtney's room. We stayed and talked for a little while and then Isaiah was excited to get to push his brother down the hallway back to our room. His little face was filled with pride and made such a precious picture. We ended up visiting Courtney and her mom later that evening as well.

All of us were released from the hospital on Tuesday. Courtney was released before us, and she asked to see Gideon one more time before leaving. She was hoping for her kids to see him too. We rolled him down to her room and got to meet her oldest son. We went back to our room, took showers, and started packing to get ready to go home. Thirty minutes have passed, and we hadn't heard back from Courtney. Then it was an hour. I told Adam that maybe I should take bags to the car or go look for food. I needed to do anything to get my mind off the what-ifs that were floating around in my brain. It was getting closer to noon. I had just finished making a salad in a to-go box when I heard back from Courtney. She apologized for the delay but said her son was really struggling with this decision. He was not much younger than Isaiah and was having trouble understanding why this baby wasn't going home with him. She was very emotional, and so was I. I sympathized with her because it's awful when our children are hurting. She said that her mom took her son downstairs and that we could come back to get Gideon.

When we walked in, she was dressed to go home and had Gideon snuggled in her arms. It was gut-wrenching because I could see the pain in her eyes. She put Gideon into his crib, and we all hugged. She had no doubt that she was doing the right thing, but that didn't take away the hurt. Adam started praying over her as we were in this circle together. We were all crying in this tender moment. Adam was praying for strength for Courtney and her boys in the coming days and in the weeks to come. He prayed for protection and understanding for her boys. He was thanking God for her heart and sacrifice. He was praising God for a mother that chose love above anything else. That moment when we were huddled together with Adam, praying over her, is forever etched in my mind. The magnitude of that moment was so intense. There we were again with our joy coming from someone else's greatest pain. You can't explain the humbleness and gratefulness that comes from that. We hugged her again and took Gideon back to our room.

Adam and I were both a wreck. It was difficult to stop crying. I was looking back at pictures from our phone recently. We took a picture right before we were discharged, and I could tell that our faces were splotchy and our eyes red from crying. We left the hospital around twelve-thirty to head home. It was another car ride full of tears. Our friends and family were excited to see our newest addition. We had people in and out over the next few weeks. Isaiah was excited to go back to school to tell his teacher about his new baby brother.

We were adjusting well to having another baby in the house. My mom came to stay with us for several days. She lives an hour away from us, so it just made sense for her to stay again. We didn't mind the help at all. Adam's parents live just a few minutes away, and it was easy for them to drop by anytime. I enjoyed being able to drop off and pick up Isaiah from school. Everything was going well. I texted Courtney off and on to give her updates and pictures. We were getting into a normal groove with our new family of four.

Chapter 17

Unexpected Hospital Stay

We took Gideon to his pediatrician for those routine checkups within the first few days and weeks after birth. Things were going well until Gideon started having trouble keeping down his feedings. It wasn't just a little spit-up either. It was projectile and a lot of it. Our pediatrician had us come in. He thought it might be reflux and instructed us to keep him elevated when he slept and directly after feedings. We tried this for a week, and it wasn't working. We went back to the pediatrician. He thought maybe he was having a reaction to the formula, so we changed to a sensitive formula. He also suggested we only feed him around an ounce at a time and then to make sure he burped well before continuing the feeding. We tried the new formula but weren't seeing any improvement.

He would vomit so badly that we would always have several pairs of clothing for him and even an extra shirt for us if we were out in public. We were constantly having to wash clothes or sheets or his car seat. After contacting the doctor again, he didn't seem too concerned because Gideon was still gaining weight and thriving. He wanted us to continue with the slow feedings, and hopefully, his stomach would adjust with time.

When Gideon was a little over a month old, I was home with him while Adam was at work. He had thrown up after every feeding that day. I called Adam in tears and told him that something wasn't right. This amount of spit-up was not normal. I even took a picture of my shirt and pants that were covered in formula. He agreed that he thought it wasn't normal and warranted another call to the pediatrician. I emailed his nurse the picture that I had taken. She said he would get back in touch with us. The next day, I had taken Isaiah to school. Adam was off on Fridays at the church, so we were just settling on the couch, when I got a phone call from our doctor. He asked if we were able to make it to Children's of Alabama hospital in Birmingham that morning as soon as possible. He wanted them to run some tests on Gideon. We said yes, quickly changed clothes, packed some items for Gideon, and left. He also told us not to feed him between now and then.

We made it to Children's around nine-thirty. We got to a waiting area for an abdominal ultrasound. While we were in this small area, Adam struck up a conversation with another mom across the way. Her son was probably around six or seven and clearly looked like he didn't feel well. She explained that he had been having lots of stomach pain and nausea but they couldn't find the root of the problem. Adam walked over to her and asked if he could pray for them. He explained that he was a minister at our church and would love to pray over them. Her entire demeanor changed because she was so touched by his kindness. I watched this worried mother hold back tears as my precious husband was praying for God to give her strength and for them to find answers and for complete healing of her son. We were in the midst of our worry over our own child, but Adam didn't miss an opportunity to bless and encourage another parent. That's also one of those moments I will never forget.

When Gideon underwent the ultrasound, I carefully watched the technician, and I could tell she kept going over one spot. She would move around this area and take pictures. My gut was telling me something was indeed wrong. She completed the ultrasound and told us she would be sending these pictures to our doctor, who would then call us back. It did not take long for us to get a phone call. We were actually still in the ultrasound room. The doctor told us that Gideon had something called pyloric stenosis that would require surgery. He apologized for not finding this sooner because this condition is rare, only affecting one in 500 babies. Most babies with pyloric stenosis don't gain weight and show signs of dehydration. Gideon wasn't showing either of those. Pyloric stenosis is an enlarged pylorus muscle that partially blocks the channel for food to pass through the small intestine into the stomach. This was why he was vomiting so much. We were told that we would not be leaving the hospital and that surgery would be scheduled that day if possible. The surgery would be done laparoscopically to loosen the tightened muscle. Wow. What a whirlwind.

Adam and I both called our moms to get help. We contacted friends and family to pray. We planned for Adam's mom to get Isaiah from school and keep him while we were at the hospital. We knew he would be happy because he loved spending time with his poppy. My mom was in Decatur, but I asked if she could go to our house to pack things for us and meet us at the hospital. Mom said absolutely, so we sent her a list of things we would need. We left the ultrasound room and headed downstairs to intake. They got us registered and sent us to our room.

Gideon had a few tests done to see if surgery would be viable for that day. One of his levels was elevated, so surgery was postponed until early Saturday morning. They also told us that he didn't need to be fed overnight. He was normally eating every three or four hours. How was he going to make it this long? He was going to be so fussy, and we couldn't do anything to comfort him. I was dreading the night ahead. They did tell us that we could dip his pacifier in sugar water about every hour. They said this normally helps soothe babies.

My mom made it to the hospital in the early evening. She ended up packing things for herself in case she needed to stay. Gideon had his own little hospital crib. We had a recliner and a couch/bench in the room. We decided it would be best if Mom could stay, and we would rotate holding Gideon in the recliner throughout the night. I was pretty sure the hospital only allows two visitors to stay overnight per room, but they made an exception for us. Gideon did well sleeping in his crib for a while. When he woke up fussy, Mom dipped the pacifier in the sugar water and held him in the recliner. He would end up spending most of the night there with his Nonnie. He did so surprisingly well. I was so worried about him being restless and upset, but he wasn't. That was definitely an answered prayer.

The nurses came by in the morning to check his levels again, and they were all normal. Surgery was on. Within the next half hour, a nurse came in again to get Gideon. They allowed one of us to walk him back to the operating room doors. Adam suggested that I do it. I will never forget that walk down the hall. The sweet nurse was so comforting because she could tell how scared I was. I silently prayed over my child that everything would go well. I gave him a kiss on the cheek and handed him off to the nurse. She explained that the operation should take less than an hour. This was another one of those times where God gives you strength in the moment. I didn't cry or freak out when I walked away after my baby was taken off to surgery.

I made it back to our room and took a shower. Mom had already gotten ready, so she and I went down to the waiting room while Adam showered. Mom and I had been sitting for less than ten minutes when a nurse popped in the room and asked for Gideon's family. She reported that everything went perfectly and we would be able to see him soon. I sent Adam a text to tell him that Gideon was already out of surgery and to hurry.

He was in the recovery room for around an hour, but we got to go to him quickly. When we saw him after surgery, his color was a little puny. The nurse showed us his abdomen where they made two tiny incisions. They used surgical glue to seal up the cuts. He was still pretty drowsy from surgery, which was normal. They told us to try to feed him shortly after he woke up. If Gideon could have several consecutive feedings without vomiting, we would get to go home!

We were so careful and methodical with his first bottle. We knew he was very hungry because it's been over twenty-four hours since he had eaten! We fed him slowly and burped him often. We kept him elevated after the feeding was over. After a few minutes, he threw up. Our hearts sank. The good news was that it wasn't projectile and the amount was definitely less than it had been. We called the nurse to tell her that he threw up. She assured us that everything would be fine and this wasn't completely out of the norm. She explained that his little belly was now able to consume all his bottle, so it would take a little time for him to adjust to being full and satisfied. He kept all his bottle down at his next feeding, but we would end up needing to spend another night in the hospital.

Gideon was quickly back to his happy and bubbly self. He was fascinated by the little light on his finger monitor when it would catch his eye. He was able to keep down all his formula at every feeding. We were discharged from the hospital on Sunday morning. We were excited to be home because my maternity leave was quickly coming to an end. I was happy to have this problem resolved before going back to work. It was a huge relief.

A Tragic Loss

Gideon continued to grow and thrive after his operation. He was hitting his milestones with each passing month. He officially became a Rogers on October 27. We continued to have a relationship with Gideon's birth mother, yet another thing we thought would never happen. We didn't see her in person, like we did with Patricia, but we did send pictures and text each other.

We celebrated his first Halloween in a true boy fashion—the brothers were Batman and Robin. We spent the week of Thanksgiving in the mountains with Adam's family and enjoyed Christmas with family and friends. The New Year passed, and everything was going great. We celebrated Isaiah's birthday on February 25. We had no idea our lives would drastically change in a matter of twenty-four hours.

We all went to work and school like normal that day. Brenda was watching Gideon at our house. We made it home after school to relieve Nana of her duties with the baby. I cooked dinner, and we were just sitting down to eat when Adam got a call from his mom. Brenda said that Jerrell, Adam's dad, hadn't come home yet from the coffee shop, a local restaurant that we all frequent. He had gone there to eat dinner and was bringing her back some food. She couldn't reach him on the phone and was concerned something had happened to him. Poppy was a severe diabetic and had multiple scares with his health. We didn't think anything would be wrong with that at this moment because he had just eaten dinner.

Adam left the house and headed toward Arley to see if, maybe, he was stuck on the side of the road somewhere. His brother, Brad, went to look for him as well. As more and more time passed, we became increasingly worried. Word had spread quickly that Jerrell was missing. People from our church and community set out canvasing the roads between the Coffee Shop and his house. Law enforcement and our fire department got involved in the search. His cell phone was pinged, and it showed that he was about twenty minutes away from his house—not in the direction of his path home. It was dark and cold. He was always cold anyway, so I knew this weather wouldn't be good for him if he was lost. Adam called me periodically with updates. I asked him if they had checked the bridge. We were surrounded by a lake, and we all had to cross a bridge to get to our houses. Did he accidentally drive into the lake? His diabetes had severely affected his vision, and it was exceptionally difficult for him to drive at night. Within an hour, nearly a hundred people were driving all over the Winston/Walker county area in search of Jerrell.

At this point, I didn't tell Isaiah anything about not knowing Poppy's whereabouts. There was no sense in getting him worried. I made sure that he couldn't see any worry or concern on my face either. All he knew was that his Daddy-O needed to go help Poppy. After the boys were in bed, I started texting or calling anyone I knew to pray. I posted on Facebook, asking for prayers. One of our volunteer firefighters, who was a church member, called Adam and Brad to tell them that they had found Jerrell.

I was sitting in the recliner, praying, when I got that call from Adam that I would never forget. He told me that George saw lights in the pond at the bottom of Nana and Poppy's road. They were taillights from Poppy's truck. He didn't make it. He evidently had driven into the pond because he couldn't see the road. I felt like the breath was knocked out of me. I started crying and told Adam that I was so sorry. I told him that I loved him, and then he had to get off the phone. He and Brad were at the location where they found their dad.

I immediately called my mom. All I could get out on the phone was, "He's gone." She started crying with me and told me that she was going to head over as soon as she could. I got out of the recliner and closed the door to Isaiah's room because I didn't want to wake him with my sobbing. Within a few minutes, I heard a knock on our garage door. It was our friends Brandon and Joy. Relief ran through my body because I wasn't alone anymore. Joy wrapped me up in a hug, and we cried together. She told me she knew that I was alone. (I have tears in my eyes as I'm typing this.) I later told Joy how much that meant to me. It's one of those moments of kindness you'll never forget.

Adam called me again to say that Brenda didn't want people coming over to her house and asked if they could come to ours. I said, "Of course."

Joy immediately started helping straighten things because she could tell I was in a bit of a panic. That was another act of love from a friend, which meant so much. She didn't ask. She just saw a need and started to help.

Adam, Brad, our new pastor (of just a few months), and several others were at the pond during this time. They were there when the dive team identified his truck and helped remove his body. I later found out that our pastor, Dr. Roger, got into the pond with his nice clothes on to help hold a tarp to cover Poppy's body so that his sons wouldn't have to see it. It was very cold that night, and he wasn't living in Arley yet. He made the almost two-hour drive home in cold, wet clothes. What a humble act in a time of need. When I was told about what Dr. Roger did, I couldn't help but cry. I got to see a tiny glimpse into his heart. That he didn't just preach the Word—he lived it. He and the others, who helped that night, didn't do it for praise and adoration. They did it because they love my family and, most importantly, because they love Jesus and live like Him. They were absolutely the hands and feet of Jesus that evening.

Within an hour, our house was filled with people. We were all in shock and heartbroken. My mom made it to the house around eleven. We had visitors for several hours. I think we finally tried to go to sleep around two-thirty. Brenda and my mom stayed in the living room together. To know Jerrell was to love him. He just oozed goodness and sincerity. He had a love for others and a passion to make heaven crowded. He rarely missed an opportunity to share Christ. He was very loved at multiple churches and around our community. This was a devastating blow to so many. Our boys thankfully slept throughout the entire night. Adam and I were dreading the morning when we would have to tell Isaiah that his beloved poppy was in heaven.

We didn't get much sleep that night. Anyone who has experienced tragedy like this knows that sleep usually evades during these times. And the manner of his death was so unsettling. I had to force my mind not to think about his suffering and struggle to escape. We let Isaiah sleep in and wake up on his own. I had talked to my principal the night before about my father-in-law being missing and that I wasn't sure if I would be at work the next day. I contacted him again with the news and told him that I didn't know when I would be back to work. I had to be here for my husband and family. Mom and Nana were taking care of Gideon when Isaiah woke up. We let him get a little breakfast and then told him that we needed to go back to the bedroom to talk.

We sat on our bed with Isaiah between us. Adam explained as gently as he could that Poppy had an accident and was no longer with us but in heaven. His reaction was gut-wrenching. I've never seen my child cry like this. It's hard enough when you yourself are hurting, but your child? That's a whole other level of pain. We knew this would be hard on Isaiah because he and his poppy had such a sweet relationship. They were best friends. They would spend hours together, piddling in his workshop and attempting to build a man cave on the farm. Isaiah loved spending the night at their house. The men would get up early to go get breakfast. They would fish together, ride the tractor, or just spend time pestering each other. They would often do this at a restaurant and would end up getting both of them in trouble. But most importantly, they loved each other immensely. It was the perfect example of a grandfather-grandson relationship.

We told Isaiah that we were going to hold onto the memories and he would get to share stories about Poppy when Gideon got older. We cried with Isaiah and held him in our bed for about half an hour. He wanted to stay in our room for a little bit before going out to the living room. I think he needed time to try and process everything before seeing his nana. We told him that he could take all the time he needed.

Brenda was sitting on the recliner when Isaiah decided to come out. He walked over to her, and they just hugged and cried. She told Isaiah that she was so sorry. Isaiah said that it was okay because he was worried about her. Then he went over to my mom, Nonnie, and hugged her and cried. I think it was good for Isaiah to have both of his grandmothers there with him during this time. I was also reminded of God's faithfulness in the midst of tragedy.

Isaiah was six months old when my dad passed away. Now Gideon was six months old when Adam's dad passed away. God's timing is perfect, and He knew that we would need these little bundles of joy to bring us light in a time filled with so much darkness.

Adam and Brad took their mother to the funeral home to work out arrangements. Their oldest brother, Brian, lived in Washington state where he was stationed in the Army. We knew a service would not be happening without him and his family. They made their way to Alabama as quickly as possible. Jerrell loved to tinker and build things. Some of his creations were beautiful. Others? Well, let's just say he got really creative sometimes, like trying to turn a pontoon into a houseboat. It wasn't pretty. One of his creations that was absolutely beautiful? His own casket. Adam and Brad got the casket out of the garage and brought it over to our house. Jerrell's sons lovingly worked on its finishing touches. They sanded it and added a light coat of varnish to add a little shine to the wood. It was simple. It would serve a purpose. It was completely Poppy.

Jerrell had served as a music minister for the majority of his life. It was just fitting to have a full choir at this service. I don't think I have ever seen so many people in our choir loft. It was another beautiful tribute to a life well lived by a faithful servant of Christ. Adam, Brad, and I also sang together at his service. Jerrell loved to hear us sing, and we knew he would want this. It was another one of the hardest times that I've had to sing, but I kept reminding myself that we were singing to honor him. I just wish I could've gotten one more hug and hear him say, "You done good, gal," after we had finished singing. He would always do that when I would sing at church. He breathed Jesus into every single thing he did. He was a man that definitely showed every fruit of the Spirit on a daily basis. My life was better because Poppy was in it. Our community and church was a better place because Jerrell was in it. His absence would be felt by so many.

Brian's family stayed in town for several days after the funeral. We all enjoyed getting to spend time together but just wished it had been under different circumstances. Brenda would end up staying at our house for the next month or so. She had just lost her husband of over fifty years. I was not about to tell her that she couldn't stay at my house. I knew that being around the boys helped bring joy during such a difficult time. Our family, being together, helped ease some of the pain in the midst of such great loss. Grief is definitely a journey, and everyone walks through it differently. It's important to give others what they need during the various stages of grief. But one thing still remains true—God will always carry us through. I love the reminder from Isaiah 46:4. "Even to your old age and gray hairs I am he, I am he who will sustain you. I have made you and I will carry you; I will sustain you and I will rescue you." Losing Jerrell was another moment that we had to rest in the arms of Jesus and let Him carry us through.

Chapter 19

God Uses Ordinary People

The following months and years would continue without any major setbacks or hardships. We were counting our blessings during that time because I knew that you are either coming out of a valley, about to go into one, or you're in the middle of one. But one thing remains true: God is there in every season of our lives. He's the God of the mountain and our ever-present help in time of need. We may not see His hand working initially, but He will reveal Himself to us in His timing. Dr. Robert Smith said in a sermon that God's delays are not God's denials. We just need to wait and trust in Him. Or we need to try to look past our trials and wait for God's response.

As I'm writing this, it is nearing the fifteenth anniversary of my shooting. Fifteen years. That seems like ages ago, but then there are moments that it seems like it was just yesterday. God protected me then and continues to do so. God uses *all* things to draw us closer to Him. Our pain is never wasted, and that was my whole intention of writing my story. I don't want mine or my family's pain to be wasted. I want people to see what happens when we stop relying on self and rely on the power of Christ alone. It was not an easy path during our adoption, but wow did He teach me so much during those years. He made beauty from my ashes, and I wouldn't change it for anything. It reminds me of the lyrics from the song "Scars" by I Am They:

> Darkest water and deepest pain
> I wouldn't trade it for anything

'cause my brokenness brought me to You
And these wounds are a story You'll use.

It's like the refiner's fire. The fire doesn't destroy. It doesn't consume completely, but it refines and purifies. He is molding us and shaping us to be more of a reflection of Him because we were created in His image. God never wanted the fires in our lives to cause destruction but refinement. In hindsight, I wish I had just listened to God sooner. But I think I would've missed out on some valuable lessons. Perhaps God uses the trials in our lives, like He did with Pharoah and the plagues in Egypt. He used the plagues to remind the children of Israel that obedience is better than sacrifice and faith is greater than fear and the power of God is unlimited. I can look back on my life and see how God has refined me during difficult seasons and not just me but my friends and family because no one ever walks through a journey alone. He has reminded me of what He *can* do when I am obedient and surrender fully to him. There is no limit to what God can do.

We all have reminders of God's faithfulness. They may be physical scars or a hospital bracelet, a mended relationship, or a baby in your arms. When we start to get discouraged, we need to look back at these reminders to know He will still be faithful to us. "Because of the Lord's great love we are not consumed, for his compassions never fail. They are new every morning; great is your faithfulness" (Lamentations 3:22–23).

Is there a burden you are carrying right now, or are you carrying your burden to God? Scripture is telling us to cast all our cares on Him, for He cares for us. We were never meant to carry burdens alone. Whatever we are going through, God is bigger. He wants us to come to Him and lay our burdens down at the foot of the cross. Only God can meet us in our deepest hurt. No one loves you the way God does. Don't be like me and think you can fix it on your own. He's waiting with open arms.

It is also my prayer that someone would come to know Christ through this book. If you've never felt that peace that I've written about, you can. God loves you so much that He sent His Son to die for you. Jesus Christ bore our sin on the cross to pay the penalty for you and for me. He led a perfect and sinless life. He gave up His throne in heaven because He saw that we were worth it. He saw our need. He not only died for us, but He was also resurrected on the third day. The grave couldn't hold the king! He made a way for you and me to be with Him in heaven one day. We must first admit that we are sinners in need of a savior. We have no power to save ourselves. We have to believe that Jesus died on the cross for our sins, was buried, and rose again. We have to confess our sin before God. We have to call upon His name to be saved and accept His gift of forgiveness. This decision is the most important one you will ever make. If you did ask Jesus to save you today, please contact me. I would love nothing more than to know that another soul was added to the flock. The angels are rejoicing over you!

"The *Lord* bless you and keep you; the *Lord* make his face shine on you and be gracious to you; the *Lord* turn his face toward you and give you peace" (Numbers 6:24–26).

A Sister's View

I was a high school math teacher at the time of Amy's trauma and was thoroughly enjoying my well-deserved summer off. Over the previous few months, my sister Amy had been staying with me a few nights a week in my apartment in Homewood, Alabama, when she had graduated school classes at the University of Montevallo. It had been a lazy Monday, and I was still in my pajama pants that afternoon. I was sitting at my desk on the computer near the front window of my apartment. It was after 4:00 p.m. I heard a horn honk. I looked outside and thought it might have been my sister's car but couldn't tell for sure as I was not wearing my glasses. (I am near-sighted and wear glasses when I drive or am in a classroom.) I didn't think anything else about it.

At 4:45 p.m., I received a phone call from an unknown number that would change our family's lives forever. It was a stranger who said my sister had been shot and was on the side of the road. He told me where she was, and it was less than five minutes from my apartment. I could hear my sister talking in the background, which I thought was a good sign. He said her car was not there. I jumped up, threw on some shoes, and ran out of the apartment as fast as I could. I called my poor boyfriend (now husband), Joseph, who was at work. I told him what had happened and asked if he would help me get in touch with my dad. While on the phone with him, I broke down after noticing what I thought was Amy's abandoned car in a parking lot across the street from Shades Mountain Baptist Church. I pulled into the parking lot quickly and saw that it was her car. I tried calling my mom but got no answer. I left a message, asking her to call back ASAP. I got in touch with Adam, Amy's husband. That was an extremely difficult call to make!

I sped down the road and found my sister, sitting up with the paramedics on the side of a grassy ditch at an odd three-way intersection. I pulled my SUV into the grass of a neighboring house and ran across the street. There was a two-inch, round bloody spot on the front of my sister's white T-shirt. I thought that must have been where the bullet went in, though I realized later that, that was where it had exited. The bullet hole was on her left abdomen about midway between her hip and breast area. She didn't appear to be in immediate pain. The paramedic said I could ride in the ambulance to the hospital.

This was my first time in an ambulance. We were not far from the best trauma hospital in the state, University of Alabama at Birmingham Medical Center; however, it was rush hour. We should have been traveling against traffic, but for some reason on that summer day, the traffic was backed up on both northbound and southbound lanes. The ambulance had to drive on the shoulder to get around the bumper-to-bumper traffic. Meanwhile, I was still frantically trying to get in touch with my family. My mom finally answered the phone. I abruptly asked her how quickly she could get to UAB. You could hear the panic in her voice as I tried to tell her what I knew at that time: Amy had been carjacked and then shot when she tried to escape.

We finally arrived at the emergency department at UAB after what seemed like forever! She was on a gurney as they wheeled her into the hospital. They allowed me to go in as far as the elevators before they whisked her away for emergency surgery. She was still talking, which was comforting, but I still had a lot of fear under the surface. They would not let me go upstairs or walk through the hospital to the emergency department waiting room. I walked out through the ambulance entrance to the outside of the building. The ER waiting room entrance was just around the corner of the building, but it seemed like the longest, loneliest walk of my life. A phone tree prayer had already been put in place to notify everyone. All our family lived at least one hour away, so I called my friend Lauren, who just lived twenty minutes away in Hoover. She couldn't believe the news and was one of the first people to make it to UAB. The front staff told me that we could go up to the surgery waiting room to get up-to-date information after her surgery. My mother's friend, Billye, worked a few blocks away at AL.com and rushed to the hospital as soon as she heard the news. It was comforting to no longer be waiting alone.

More and more people started filling the waiting room as the hours progressed. Some of my dear church family arrived quickly that evening. Their prayers and presence were coveted. Adam and his dad arrived, and I tried to relay what I knew. The hours kept on going by, and we hadn't heard anything about Amy's progress. They finally came out to give us an update. The bullet had been shot from the back and had gone straight through. In the process, she had lost her spleen and her kidney, which are both expendable organs. Unfortunately, the bullet nicked her pancreas, which could become problematic, but overall, things could have been a lot worse!

We finally got to see her later that night, just a few of the family at a time. She was hooked up to tubes and a breathing apparatus, so she could not talk. She was feverishly trying to use sign language to communicate with us, but we do not know sign language. It was gut-wrenching. We only had a few minutes with her until she was moved to the trauma ICU on the ninth floor. I left the room crying. Adam, my family, and Joseph stayed the night in the large ICU waiting room. Some of the long-haulers in the waiting room had already staked out the long benches that could double as a makeshift bed. So we did the best we could to catch a little sleep by putting some chairs together. After one difficult ICU visiting hour, I remember our group praying together. We just never knew how each ICU visit would be.

Amy's case had made the news. Even though Birmingham has a lot of crimes, a young woman getting carjacked is not an everyday occurrence. She was abducted in my apartment complex in the city of Homewood but had tried to escape the vehicle and, subsequently, had been shot two miles down the road in Hoover. There were multiple police municipalities working on the case. We met with the Hoover detectives on the second floor in the large main lobby at UAB. They asked lots of questions. I told them I thought I had seen

Amy's car outside my car when I heard a car horn but couldn't tell if anyone was in it. I told him the location of my sister's car. He said that there was a car with two other individuals, which trailed behind Amy's car. She was not the only person they had robbed/carjacked that night. They officers promised to keep us up-to-date on the investigation as things progressed.

Even though I had an apartment about twenty minutes away, we did not want to leave the hospital so we could stay close to Amy (plus I was a little nervous about going back there). That first week in the hospital was full of uncertainty about her health status. She was still in the ICU and only had visiting hours for an hour or two a day. We had claimed our own spot in the waiting room at this time and had gotten to know and pray with some of the other families there. I remember a few of the patients had suffered from motorcycle accidents. Family and friends would come to visit during the week. My dad was able to come down on Tuesday. We had cookies, edible arrangements, and all sorts of things brought to the hospital by concerned family and friends. One of Joseph's gifts is being able to make people laugh, especially when things are stressful and tense. He told Adam a joke about Mike Tyson that we *still* laugh about! Adam repeated that joke to probably half the people that came to visit! It was hilarious, hearing him get so cracked up each time.

We found out from a fellow waiting room dweller that UAB has some small apartments/rooms nearby that were available for family members of patients. We talked to a few people and were finally able to secure a room. The place was called UAB Townhouse and was located a few blocks from the hospital building where Amy was located. The room did not look like it had been updated since the late '70s, but it had two twin beds, a recliner, and a kitchenette and would be home away from home for the next week or so. We took turns on who would stay at the hospital with Amy and who would get to sleep in a bed. Several nights, we put the twin beds on the floor to make a giant king bed so several of us could sleep on the bed. Dad camped out in the recliner one night. I was even able to make sausage balls (a family favorite) in the tiny oven in the kitchenette one day. The walk to Amy's part of the hospital was not bad during the day, but we preferred not to walk outside after dark. We were able to find a pathway through several of the UAB hospital buildings, so we only had to walk one block outside.

Meanwhile, Amy had been moved to a regular room. The morphine they had her on in the beginning made her very hot, which was unusual for her, and she kept the hospital room at what seemed like just a few degrees above freezing. She had drains coming out her back and chest. She was starting to move around a little more. The detectives had come in to discuss a few things about the case. A little while later, Amy was feeling well enough and agreed to do a press conference with Adam. They both said they were praying for the people who did this to her. Adam said they forgave them for what they had done. The whole scene seemed surreal. My sister was on the news and doing a press conference. I had a reporter from the *Birmingham News* contact me about what happened to Amy. Representatives from a few national crime and daytime talk shows contacted Adam, wanting to talk with them about Amy's story, but he politely declined.

The following week, Amy was still in the hospital and seemed to not be doing well, though she was actually a little better. I was supposed to report back to work for teacher in-service days. My very understanding principal, Jane Baker, let me stay on leave for the first week of school since everything with Amy's health was still uncertain. At this time, I still had not stayed back at my apartment and didn't really care to. My roommate had gotten married while Amy was in the hospital. Our lease had already expired without us knowing. The gracious landlord let us move out of the apartment without advance notice because of all that had happened.

While Amy was still in the hospital, we found out from the Hoover and Homewood police departments that the carjackers had been caught. The Hoover detectives explained that there were three people involved in the crime. A young, large, Black man was the person who pulled a gun on my sister and forced her into the passenger seat while she was trying to get out of the car. A thirty-year-old woman trailed behind them with an even younger man with her in the getaway car. The carjacker wanted to take Amy to an ATM to withdraw money, we learned.

Amy's physical body still had a long way to heal, but the physicians recognized she needed help mentally as a victim of such a violent crime. A caseworker informed Amy that there was an organization that offered special counseling and benefits to victims of violent crimes. Amy was able to get counseling after discharging home from the hospital. Mental healing was going to take a lot longer than physical healing. Naturally, she did not want to drive by herself, stay with me in my new apartment, or be by herself at home. A lot of these fears she was able to face over time.

This was one of the most traumatic times of my life. The true terror that something like this could happen to my sister right outside my apartment in a supposedly safe part of town was hard to believe. The unknowns in those first hours and days were so tough: Would Amy make it? Would the perpetrators who were at large retaliate at my apartment? What quality of life would Amy have if she did make it?

Despite all these difficult times, we had a lot of fond memories of time spent with family and friends in the waiting room and, eventually, in Amy's hospital room, like telling jokes to make my granddaddy snicker, singing jingles from commercials, drawing pictures to decorate Amy's hospital room (which became *covered* in cards, pictures, and notes), Adam telling the Mike Tyson joke a hundred times. So many people were so considerate and generous. A local biker group heard about Amy's story and held a fundraiser for her medical bills. Neither Amy nor Adam are bikers and had no connection with this group. This was just something they felt that they needed to do. Tragic situations tend to bring the best and worst out in people. We saw more of the best of people during this time.

I am so thankful to God for saving my sister. The outcome could have been much different if the bullet had strayed just a centimeter to the left through her pancreas. God has already used her story to bring about His glory. We won't know why this happened on this side of heaven. But I do know that Amy and our family are stronger because of it.

"For I consider that the sufferings of this present time are not worthy to be compared with the glory that is to be revealed to us" (Romans 8:18).

"And we know that God causes all things to work together for good to those who love God, to those who are called according to His purpose" (Romans 8:28).

Amy's work is not finished on earth. God has a plan for her life that is so much better than even she can imagine. Thank God for His gracious love and for giving me more time with my sister.

A Husband's View

On July 31, 2006, my life with my wife of only nine months started like every other day, but what would take place a few short hours later would shake the foundations of not only our lives but also the lives our family, our church, our friends, and several communities.

I'm writing this testimony mostly from my view, since it is what I lived and remember best. For the last year or so leading up to this day, my wife has been getting her fifth-year degree in elementary education at the University of Montevallo. During that summer term of classes, Amy had worked it out with her sister, Lanae, to stay a few nights a week at her gated apartment complex located not far off Lakeshore Avenue in Birmingham. Amy was arriving at that apartment complex after classes on that clear, hot, and muggy afternoon.

At around four-thirty, as I was getting home from work, unknown to me, my wife was going through the most scary and horrific ordeal of her life. At about four-fifty, I had just taken out the trash and walked back into our house to see that, in those few short minutes, I had missed six phone calls from Lanae.

Thinking this kind of odd, I gave Lanae a quick call back, little knowing that the next six words I would hear from my sister-in-law would be the start of an incredible, God-ordaining, and God-sustaining story that we will never forget and that we will tell for years to come.

Those six words? "Adam, Amy's been carjacked and shot!"

My mind immediately jumped to a mindset that said, "This has to be a joke," but I was quickly drawn into Lanae's next words—"we are in an ambulance on our way to UAB hospital!"

It was then that I could hear sirens blazing and paramedics working on Amy in the background.

I quickly hung up with Lanae, my mind racing, and grabbed my keys and wallet and headed out the door while calling my mom and dad to see if Daddy would drive me to the hospital because I knew I was in no shape mentally and physically to drive. About two minutes later, I skidded into their rock driveway where Daddy and I switched places, and we took off the hour's drive to Birmingham.

A few minutes later after talking again quickly with Lanae, I learned that Amy had been shot in the back with the bullet exiting through her diaphragm out the front of her lower chest. Lanae said that Amy had somehow never lost consciousness (God!) and was talking with the doctor and nurses as they were wheeling her into surgery.

I found out later that Amy was making a joke about the accent of her British surgeon as they were prepping her. What a great God we serve that He would create our bodies in a way that even during a tragic event, we go into shock mode with so much adrenaline that even twenty to thirty minutes after being shot and not really knowing whether she might live or die, God was holding her in His hands while she made jokes. Praise the Lord Jesus, our great God and creator!

That hour-long ride was filled with a lot of questions, a lot of phone calls, a lot of anxiety, and a lot of prayers. The main one at that time was to survive the trip to the hospital. Daddy, who had what I would call a remarkable God-calm about him, was driving quickly to say the least, but then as we neared Sumiton on the old Seventy-eight Highway to Birmingham, we ran into a huge, summer-afternoon, five-minute-long downpour—the kind where you can't see your hand in front of your face.

Then after finally getting through that, we were blue-lighted by an officer on a motorcycle near Adamsville. Thankfully, he just pulled up beside us at a red light, and after we quickly told him what was happening, he just reminded us to slow down so we would make it there in one piece.

After what seemed like an eternity, Daddy wheeled into the emergency room at UAB, and I jumped out, and I ran into the hospital that would basically be our home for the next month. I had yet to get to talk to Amy or know that they had taken her back for exploratory surgery to see the damage from the bullet. Once I located Lanae in the waiting room, my tears started once again, not knowing whether Amy would survive through the surgery. My mind raced back to try to remember the last thing I had said to her that morning as she left the house.

At that point early on, it was just Daddy, Lanae, and I, along with some church friends of Lanae's, in the waiting room, but as 6:00 p.m. came and went and then 7:00 p.m., word continued to spread, and the waiting room began to fill up with family, coworkers, and church friends from literally all over Alabama. We learned later that prayers were being lifted up over the country. I would say that by the time 8:00 p.m. rolled around, there were around ninety people covering that entire room, waiting for a word from the doctors on Amy.

It was, without a doubt, a very stressful time, watching as all the news stations were carrying live coverage of what had happened and then to see helicopter footage of Amy's car, sitting all alone in a church parking lot, where the carjacker had dumped her car. And all this time, we still did not know much at all about Amy's condition and whether she would survive.

As bad as everything sounded and looked, even in or, should I say, especially in the midst of that dark valley, my Lord and savior was holding me up. My eyes are watering as I write this, remembering back to that day and, at that time, not really understanding what was going on in my spirit. There was just no way to describe it because the entire time in that waiting room, and in the days to come, as crazy and illogical as this sounds, I had no animosity or hate toward those who did this to my wife. It was probably the first time in my twenty-five-year-old life that I had truly experienced God's "peace that passes all understanding."

I'll be honest, it was to the point that I wondered if there was something wrong with me—that I didn't want to go get my own guns and go looking for those who did this and go take care of them myself. But in God's infinite wisdom and me knowing Romans 8:28 that "in *all* things, God works for the good of those who love Him and are called according to His purpose," I knew that God had a plan and a purpose for this chapter in our lives and that all Amy and I wanted was for Him to get *all* the glory and honor He so rightly deserves and for us to just be obedient to His plan.

The surgeon came out around eleven-thirty that night after six hours of surgery and said that the bullet passed through her left kidney and spleen, nicked her pancreas, and then came out through her diaphragm between two ribs but, miraculously, had not bounced around hitting any other organs. He continued to say that he removed Amy's left kidney and spleen but expected her to not only live but also eventually make a full recovery (praise God)!

All these later—after many days and nights in the hospital, a few months of packing bullet wounds, and several months of emptying drainage tubes, as well as many trips to the best Christian counselor we could've ever hope for, my wife today, to the glory of God, is:

1. not dead,
2. not paralyzed,
3. can live without the organs they had to remove, and
4. doesn't even have to take medicine on a daily basis!

That is the God I serve!

To sum it up, please know that both Amy and I pray, hope, beg, and plead that someone who has heard her speak over the years or watched her testimony on YouTube or who may be reading this right now may feel the Holy Spirit knocking at your heart's door. Maybe you've maybe never understood who God is or that He wants to be in your life. Please message us or get in touch with us so that we can share with you what it means to have a relationship with the God who created you!

Proverbs 3:5–6 reads, "Trust in the Lord with all your heart and lean not on your own understanding. But in all your ways acknowledge Him and He will direct your path."

The year 2006 was a life-changing year for me. In January, I had started as a quality assurance assistant at a company in Johnson City, Tennessee. This was my first position in the cooperative education (co-op) program through the University of Alabama in Huntsville (UAH) and took the place of the second semester of my sophomore year. Then for summer school, I enrolled in some challenging courses. Little did I know how much would happen that summer.

In early July, I began to feel extremely lethargic. My tonsils were swelling, and I was running a fever. The urgent care doctor took one look in my mouth and asked me if I had been able to eat that day. Apparently, my tonsils were so swollen that they were touching each other. She ordered strep throat and mononucleosis tests, and I awaited the results. Strep: negative, but mono: positive! I was shocked, as my girlfriend wasn't sick, and I hadn't shared any drinks or water fountains with anyone recently. I was sent home with a corticosteroid prescription and was told to rest and plan on being tired and sick for several weeks.

Sure enough, it was the most miserable three weeks of illness I had ever experienced. I was barely able to get out of bed most days. I had just built a new PC, which was conveniently located in my bedroom, so I watched a lot of TV. My parents were great to bring me stew or soup so I could at least try to eat something other than crackers and water.

After three agonizing weeks, I was finally feeling well enough to return to classes. I had missed three weeks of my five-week US history course but had been in constant communication with my professors about my illness, so he said I could make up the work during the second five-week course. My other professors had similarly offered to let me make up the work before the end of the summer semester, so I was buckled down for an intense time as I packed the coursework of a regular semester into five weeks.

Earlier in July, I had been very sick with mono. Due to a slow recovery, I missed several weeks of school and finally was able to return to class towards the end of the month. My professors were helpful in allowing me to make up work but I had a time line in which to finish it all. It was an intense time with make up work as well as regular coursework, getting crammed into just a few weeks. July 31, 2006 was a Monday that started like any other that summer. I woke up late, still weak and tired but headed to the four classes I had that day. My last course of the day, intro to probability, was to end around 7:30 p.m. I was still a bit weak and tired from mono but had made it through a whole week already, so I could handle another, right? The day was uneventful until my last course of the day: intro to probability. As the professor was describing the various permutations of a roll of two fair dice, my dad called my cell phone. He often called at random points in the day, sometimes to talk about dinner plans or sometimes to ask for a favor. I ignored the call and tried to focus on the professor. Dad called again. Pretty irritated, I ignored the call again and texted him that I was in class. Dad didn't really text at all, so I wasn't expecting a response, but he at least knew how to read them. Problem solved, now back to focusing on lecture—

Then Joseph called me. Joseph was dating my eldest sister, Lanae, and he rarely ever called me, but I still thought nothing of it. I ignored the call and texted him to say I was trying to focus on class. He texted me back, "Leave class now and call me."

I replied with, "I already missed three weeks of class this summer. I can't, or I will fail."

Boy, did I *not* expect what popped on my phone a few seconds later: "Andrew, Amy has been shot. She's going to UAB. Get down here now."

My heart sank. I felt a chill run down my spine and all the color run right out of my skin. I hurriedly packed up my things, far noisier than I intended, threw on my backpack, and called Joseph back as I ran out the door. I remember my professor saying to the class, "I don't know what that was about, but whatever it is, I guess he'll let me know later," and then he chuckled and got back to his lecture.

As I rushed down the stairs, Joseph picked up and began telling me about Amy being shot outside Lanae's apartment, how Lanae was rushing to the hospital with her, and how I just needed to go get my dad and get to Birmingham as quickly as possible. I was about forty minutes from my dad's house, assuming I went the speed limit. Twenty-seven minutes later, I screamed into his driveway and rushed inside. Immediately, I could tell that he had already been drinking, and my anxiety boiled over into pure rage. I poured his drink down the kitchen sink and told him to get his shoes on. We were going to Birmingham immediately, and I was realizing that I had to be the one to drive.

Rage has a way of making you forget, so the next thirty to sixty minutes were a bit of a blur. I distinctly recall my cousin Alison running interference and batting down every excuse my dad had for not leaving immediately. Dad was obviously ashamed of his alcoholism and seemed sure that the ninety minutes to UAB wouldn't be enough to sober him up. He, of course, did not use those words. Instead, he made excuses about not being able to sleep in a waiting room because of his bad back, needing to smoke in the car but all of us not liking that, and even his responsibilities at the family store the next day. All were trivial things that we, as a family, would obviously help resolve, and Alison was having *none* of it from him. Alison was even saying she should drive him home since she couldn't spend the night either. Our efforts were futile because he ended up not going to the hospital.

I think either Alison or my uncle Joe and aunt Dianne took me to the hospital. We arrived at the UAB parking garage. This would be my first time of many trips over the next couple of weeks. We rushed into the ICU waiting room and saw Adam, my mom, Lanae, and several other friends and family members anxiously awaiting more news about Amy. We prayed together. We listened as Lanae and Adam pieced together what they could about the events that had just transpired. We prayed some more—for the doctors, for Amy, for God's protective hands to envelop Amy and keep her safe.

After a few anxious hours in the waiting room, we got news that Amy was in critical but stable condition. There was a lot of medical jargon that my twenty-year-old brain didn't understand, but the doctors tried to comfort us as much as they could. The bullet had missed her lungs and heart by fractions of an inch but had caused damage to other organs. It would be a long road to recovery, but she should make it through. Praise the Lord!

After a few nights at the hospital, we ended up being housed in the UAB dorms for the night, and I ended up in a room with Dad, Lanae, and Joseph. Joseph and I pulled extra mattresses, if you could even call them such, to the floor and tried to fall asleep. Joseph and Lanae had been together long enough for me to know that he was a character and that sleeping next to him for the night was going to be interesting. Joseph is a big guy, having played on the offensive line in high school and college, and was cracking jokes and trying to lighten the mood as we settled in for the night. Seven or so hours of bad sleep later, I heard the others stirring and started to wake up. As I lifted my head from the pillow, Joseph yelled, "*Steamrollerrrr*," and rolled his three hundred-pound body over mine, immediately squeezing the air from my lungs as Lanae looked on and laughed at us. Then he rolled back over me again! If that doesn't get your blood flowing in the morning, nothing will!

The first few days were an emotional roller coaster as we received bad news about Amy losing organs and then good news that the surgeries went well and no vital organs had been damaged. I recall one doctor telling us that there could hardly be a more perfect path for a bullet to take through a human body. I firmly believe that God guided Amy into the perfect position to save her life when she made the courageous decision to jump out of the car.

I was able to visit Amy several times over the next week, but visitation hours and the number of people allowed back were both extremely limited while she was in the ICU. As people visited, they began leaving small tokens from the outside world to make the hospital room seem less desolate: flowers, cards, crayon drawings from our cousins and other kids who loved Amy dearly. I'm not much of an artist, but I was dead broke after having missed three weeks from my restaurant job, so I decided to take on the difficult task of recreating *Teen Girl Squad* from the *Strong Bad Emails* series on *Homestar Runner*. (If you have no idea what that is, please do yourself a favor and go look it up. It perfectly encapsulates the weird, deadpan humor of youths of the mid-2000s unlike anything else I can think of.)

After Amy was awake and alert, I proudly presented my drawing to her, knowing how much she enjoyed the silly little stick drawing cartoon and did my best impression of the girls. She laughed and immediately winced in pain, so I apologized and taped it to the wall with all the other drawings and cards. She thanked me for the laugh, even though it hurt, and asked me to do the voice often when I visited in the hospital.

Conversations with victims of violent crime and trauma are never easy, and I had no idea what to talk about while I was in there, even with my own sister. I just shared stories from my first semester in Tennessee, the shenanigans I had been getting into with my friends back home, and memories of visiting her at UNA after I got my license and could drive to see her myself. Any time she winced or tried to move, I tried to help or offered to get a nurse for her. I was pretty much useless, but I had to at least try something.

One day while I was visiting her, Amy had to drink a contrast drink to get ready for some sort of imaging to be done. She did her best to chug it as the nurse kindly but firmly urged her on until she finished the whole thing. Not long after the nurse left, Amy got a queasy look on her face and said, "Andrew, I need a—" and I immediately sprang to my feet just in time for her to vomit the colored liquid and stomach bile all over herself. I rushed out to get a nurse to help and did what I could to aid them before they asked me to just step in the hallway so they could get her changed.

As Amy's situation improved and her recovery seemed ever more certain, the waiting room transformed from an anxious, quiet space of heavy emotion into the loud, jovial atmosphere that I was accustomed to with my family. One day, Joseph told Adam a joke: "What's Mike Tyson's phone number?" "Fee fi fo, fee fi fo fo." I'm not sure what precisely about that joke tickled Adam so much, but you could just see a million pounds of burden lift from his shoulders as he let loose a big belly laugh. Every new person who visited the hospital was a new opportunity for Adam to share the joke again, so I can't even tell you how many times I heard it. To this day, I can't see a picture of Mike Tyson without thinking of Adam and how much he loved that joke during those weeks. Sometimes, God works through words of wisdom or feelings of peace, and other times, He's simply present in a good joke.

The limited hours for visitation also left us with a lot of time to kill during the day, especially when many people were there to visit her. Dad and I would go explore the hospital complex and the surrounding areas when we were both there. I recall a walk to the cafeteria and just talking about how lucky we were to have Amy still with us and to have a support system to grant us breaks like that one to decompress and get out of the stale environment of an ICU waiting room.

On another break, I was walking with my stepdad Mike, Joseph, and Lanae. As we walked by Pete's Famous Hot Dogs, Joseph jokingly mentioned the restaurant's name, to which Mike responded, "You ain't ever heard of Pete's Famous Hot Dogs?" with the incredulous tone of an authoritative hot dog connoisseur.

Joseph asked him, "No, are they any good?"

Mike said, "Don't know. I've never tried 'em!"

Joseph and I nearly fell out on the sidewalk from laughing. There were many bleak times in those days and weeks, but I have held tightly to the positive memories. They remind me of God's promise to always walk with us and never forsake us if we trust in Him.

I don't recall the exact time I got back home or returned to classes that summer, but I know I've missed enough of the semester that I could not complete any of my classes to the point where I could receive grades. I returned to classes as I could and visited the hospital often on my lighter days and the weekends. It was so heart-warming to see Amy's room more vibrant and decorated each time I visited, as more people dropped off cards, drawings, and flowers. Around the time that Amy was discharged from the hospital, I had to move back to Tennessee to start my second semester of work in the co-op program. Thankfully, Amy's situation had improved dramatically, so I felt comfortable being so far away from the family as life began to return to its new state of normal.

The following semester was intense, as I traveled back and forth from Tennessee to Alabama to take makeup exams, complete programming assignments, and turn in papers for the classes that I had not been able to complete over the summer, all while working forty hours as a QA developer, writing automated tests for a product that I barely understood. One of my professors had left the university at the end of the summer, which made things even more difficult. I ended up petitioning the dean of the college of science to allow me to make the class up with a new professor, instead of dealing with an uncooperative former employee. After hearing my story in its entirety, he simply changed my grade to an A and wished me luck in the rest of my education. Even with all the added stress they brought, I was happy to make all those trips as it meant that I could check in with my family often and get frequent updates about Amy's recovery.

A traumatic event like a violent crime forever changes a family. Each person close to Amy has a story like this. We remember where we were when we first heard the news. We can still feel the anxiety, the anger, the fear over what had been done to her and what awaited her in the minutes, hours, days, and weeks to come. There were two big things that gave me comfort through the entire experience: (1) that Amy was saved, and no matter what happened, I would see her smile and give her a hug again in heaven and (2) that my family, despite our many faults, would rise to the occasion and support each other emotionally, physically, mentally, and financially.

When God remains first in your heart and mind, you experience a peace that transcends understanding. When a community keeps God first, they do works that accomplish a greater good than any one person could accomplish alone and let the glory of God shine on all those that they care for. It's my prayer that this story touches someone and leads them to a new relationship with Christ or a deepening of their existing relationship with Him.

> Consider it pure joy, my brothers and sisters, whenever you face trials of many kinds,

because you know that the testing of your faith produces perseverance. Let perseverance finish its work so that you may be mature and complete, not lacking anything. (James 1:24)

A Mother's View

"How quick can you get to UAB? Amy's been shot," was how my daughter's saga started for me.

That day is etched in the hearts and minds of our family, just as are the day JFK was assassinated and the 9/11 attacks. It was a day that changed everything.

On Monday, July 31, 2006, I lived with my husband Mike's granny, who had Alzheimer's, and I had been sick most of the day. When Mike got in from work, I asked him to come sit with her as I felt that if I could just sleep for an hour, I would feel better. He had been there about thirty minutes when my cell rang in the other room. It was my daughter Lanae's ringtone, but I was just finally resting good, so I let it go, figuring—as we always do—if it's important, she'll call back. Well, she called back!

"How quick can you get to UAB?" was the first thing she said, which took me from a prone position to a standing one in less than two seconds. The next words made my knees go weak—"Amy's been shot!"

"*What?* What did you say? How? Where?" and Lanae began to tell me, most of which I misheard as I was up thinking, moving, making a plan. I had to get to UAB Medical Center! All I remember is that she said she was shot in the chest, and I thought she said the guy got her at an exit and pulled her out of the car, which, in my mind, meant she would surely die. In reality, she probably said the guy carjacked and shot Amy as she jumped out of the car. Lanae had to hurry since she was on her way to the scene, as Amy wasn't far from her, and I was to meet them at UAB. My first words to Mike had to be shocking to him as well. I just blurted, "Amy's been shot! I have to go! You need to call your mother to come stay with

Granny! I've got to change clothes! I've got to call people—we've got to *hurry*!" I am thinking of people I need to call. I have to get to the basement and get my bra out of the washer! My mind was racing as fast as my heart. Funny, the little things you remember. I had on a red bandana top and black shorts. Since that day, every time I see a red bandana, I think of Amy's incident.

Everything I thought I would need, I found and got it together before Mike's mother, Caroyldean, got there and we could leave. Sometime in all this, we got some misinformation that she was just shot in the leg, and I felt relief, thinking that even if she lost a leg, that's no big deal—she could wear a prosthesis. I shared the false information with my mother, who took her time getting to the hospital because I never called to correct it.

My first phone call was to my friend Billye Asherbranner. She worked in downtown Birmingham at that time, and I knew she could get there before we could—and Lanae was there alone as she rode in the ambulance with Amy. She did *not* need to be there alone if at all possible! Billye got to her first—and I am so thankful for that!

Once we were on our way, I called two of the best prayer warriors I knew—Julie Widick and Margie Jones Alexander. Julie has been a good, faithful, and strong friend since the '80s, and Margie and I were thrown together when we worked at Hartlex Antiques. Friends, if you don't know the power of prayer, then you need to come to know Jesus and see for yourself just how it works! When the Bible speaks of a peace that passes all understanding, that was *exactly* what we all felt that night. I honestly cannot explain it. *Yes*, there was fear, especially when we discovered the bullet had gone all the way through her and exploratory surgery was necessary. We had gotten misinformation again that the wounds were superficial but then began wondering why it was taking so long. Three hours passed, then four, then five…

Oh, how thankful I was for a waiting room *full* of people. They were dusty, dirty people, who had been out, mowing fields, when they got the call, people in their work uniforms, people with office attire, family who drove a couple of hours to be here as support, all who loved Amy and were there to support Adam and the rest of us.

All those people helped to comfort us with our chitchat, talk about family and friends, and an Alabama versus Auburn rivalry jab here and there—most all, who could stay until she was out of surgery, which was after 11:00 p.m. Prior to that, the local news came on in a small area of the waiting room, and the first video footage of what was now our surreal life was on the ten o'clock news. Of course, many details were missing, as they would be for a few days. But I can remember standing there, in an empty corner section of the waiting room (empty because all the chairs had been moved to the main area), surrounded by my nephew Joey Russell and his parents, Dianne and Joe, watching an unfamiliar newscaster talk about *our* Amy—you know, the kind of thing we watch every day but always somebody else. Now it was us. And that was weird.

The news folks had questions, and so did we! When we learned it was a carjacking, we could *not* figure why they would want her car, as it was a 1998 Nissan Altima. One clue the police had was one Amy gave them—that a silver late model Camry was behind them, probably a 2004. (She had been car hunting, and that model was a favorite.) It also had lots of stuffed animals in the back window. We knew that Amy had a lot of answers to our questions—she just had to make it through the surgery and recovery.

Once she was out of surgery, we met in a large conference room and got the info from the surgeon about what had happened. I was *so* glad I was sitting down, as when the surgeon started to list the organs that they removed or that were nicked, my head was spinning a bit. None of that sounded superficial to me! Don't you *need* both kidneys? Don't you *need* your spleen? And that pancreas? I *know* it's essential to life. What does nicking mean? I believe the information we had heard earlier using the word superficial. It probably meant "expendable organs," ones that you *can* live without. Superficial to me meant a flesh wound—or maybe, in this case, since the bullet went all the way through, it just left a pathway to patch! Lord, have mercy. That was either totally dense thinking or just hopeful thinking! He said that it was good that the bullet was a .38 and not a .22, as it went straight through. A .22 would have bounced around and done damage they couldn't repair without her bleeding out. It missed her spine by less than an inch or so, damaged her left kidney and her spleen, so they removed them. It also nicked her pancreas, so that involved a separate drain to keep infection down. It would eventually be that pancreas that kept her in the hospital for so long. So for the type of gunshot it was, it *did* do the least amount of damage to a body, and that body still survived!

No matter. She made it through surgery, and we could see her. We were *not* adequately prepared for that first visit, *that* is for certain. Adam and I went in. My word! My beautiful daughter wasn't recognizable because of swelling due to the long surgery. Her eyes were swollen shut, a ventilator tube was taped to her face, and her lips were turned almost inside out. Her hands were tied down so she wouldn't pull out any of the tubes—they were everywhere. An ugly, thick PICC line bulged from her neck. I am *so* very thankful that she was asleep when we first came in because I don't think we could have masked our expressions at that time.

Adam called her name, and she opened her eyes as best she could. She tried talking but couldn't. Adam talked to her sweetly, gently. We had tears flowing. Amy moved her hands and realized she was tied down. Tears edged their way down her cheek. She started to move her hands again, and we realized she was using sign language, the alphabet, to communicate. But in that moment, while I knew the alphabet, I wasn't remembering anything past A, E, and the "I love you" hand sign! We couldn't stay long; her nurse had us leave. (The trauma unit has one nurse per patient.) We were to come back during the first visiting hour—of which there were only four or five each day. We cried our way back to the waiting room, but they were also tears of joy too, praises to God sent up that she was *alive*! Everything seemed hopeful and good. By that time, not too many were still in the waiting room since most left after we shared the surgeon's news after the surgery.

A trauma waiting room is somewhat different than a regular ER waiting room. The people/family there are experiencing some horrific, unexpected events. You sort of make camps. It becomes a mini home away from home with blankets, sheets, and pillows, maybe a cooler, a basket of snacks and fruit, and sacks from McDonalds and other places. After having received blankets and pillows from the hospital, we made our camp and decided we needed to try to get some sleep. All the other camps were asleep, but we honestly could not sleep. The word *excitement* holds many meanings, and it was probably what kept us up—leftover adrenaline, I was sure! So here were four adults—Adam, Lanae, Andrew, and me—all giggling over stupid things, trying to figure the scenarios that happened from the bits of info we had been given by the police, knowing that we needed to shut up because those other families needed their rest. Well, that was for naught because, somehow, the alarm system kept going off, making sleep impossible for everyone!

We finally did doze off, only to start the day over with visits to see Amy and with Adam dealing with the media person at the hospital, who was getting constant calls from the TV stations, wanting to interview him. (*What?*) Flowers were delivered from the US Marshals. (*What?*) Police officers were there (and had been earlier during the surgery). An FBI agent was there too. (*What!*) The surreal just got more surreal. We can most assuredly say we learned a lot about crime solving, federal agencies, federal laws, and so much more during this—things we would have rather left unbeknownst to us. But well, here we were. We learned that the US Marshals are almost always involved or at least offer their services when firearms are involved. The FBI was involved because carjacking is also kidnapping, which is a federal crime.

We did have so many questions—and many, Amy had answered when she was interviewed by the police, as she was fully conscious until they put her out for the surgery. We learned that her captor hadn't set out to hurt her; he just wanted money. But who was he? And who was in the other car?

Amy's story was front-page news back home—main headlines. It was also front page in the *Birmingham News*—more surreal times. The *Decatur Daily* and *Birmingham News* had called, wanting a picture of Amy, and all I could find that I could email was one from her wedding. People began calling. Even the shop owners where I had an antique booth in Hoover called to say, "We saw you on the news— how are you related to the girl who got carjacked and shot?"

We had reports from people, saying they couldn't believe that they were seeing Amy's picture in every newsstand box. One of the most touching calls was from her former band/percussion director, Clay Sloan, who said he cried when he read the paper. The mom of one of Amy's old boyfriends wrote a card, saying that when she got her news, she went to her porch and sat and cried. Knowing that your child made an impact on these and many other people, enough to share such a personal moment, is humbling and, well, if you knew Amy growing up, somewhat mind-blowing. After all, most of my stories of child-raising start with, "There was this one time that Amy—"!

Amy's dad, Danny, and I had another mind-blowing moment. Amy was at the end of her first semester at Montevallo and had one or two finals left during the week after she was shot. One of her professors came to visit us at the hospital and let us know that she and the others had talked with the school president and, given her grades, felt she would have made an A on the final, so that was what they were giving her. The professor may have mistaken our dropped jaws as due to gratitude, but really, it was shock because no teacher had ever mentioned Amy's name and "given her grades, she gets an A" in the same sentence—*not ever*, not in thirteen years of elementary, middle, and high school and not in five years at the University of North Alabama. Amy was the proverbial B/C average student. We collected our jaws and thanked her for coming to visit and giving us the good news. We found ourselves still sitting down from the sheer shock. Once she was out of earshot, we both said at the same time, "Did she say what I thought she said about Amy's grades?" I will have to say Montevallo's staff was top-notch. The president called more than once to check on us, shift Amy's schedule, and much more. Later, when she returned to class, several instructors gave up their parking spots so she could park closer to the school, as not to walk as far in the dark after class!

Amy's ventilator stayed in for another day, and her UNA college friend Allison brought us an American sign language chart so we could make out some of what she was trying to say. Most were things we couldn't fix, like taking out the tube and removing her restraints. We were told she would be in that unit until at least Friday, so the hospital set us up at the UAB Townhouse so we could rest better. By this time, Joseph, Lanae's boyfriend, had joined us, and he always makes a sad situation lighter! We again giggled, shared memories, decided that Rick and Bubba radio hosts needed to talk to Amy (Joseph got their number!) and didn't sleep near likely than we needed to. But it felt like rest because we had less worry—it seemed.

That Wednesday, we had a flurry of excitement—the doctors had decided Amy had improved enough to be moved to regular ICU! That was more proof of powerful prayers! It also meant the ventilator was gone and we could stay with her around the clock!

This began what would be the most emotionally trying part for us. You would think the horror of hearing "has been shot" or "lost a kidney, her spleen" would be the hardest of such feelings. As I said before, we all had that peace that cannot be described in an area where there was much agony and pain. In the waiting room, we learned agonizing stories of family, who had been hurt in tragic accidents, most with dire futures. We shared stories, hugged, and promised to pray for one another.

One day, probably that same Wednesday, we were in the elevator, leaving to go eat between visits. We recognized a lady from being in one of the camps, and she asked us who we were with. Adam told her, and she was so surprised! She had heard about Amy in the news and knew she was here but couldn't figure out which one was her family because no one was crying or angry or doing the things she expected from a crime victim's family. So right there in that elevator, Adam told her about that peace we have and that, even if the Lord would have called Amy home, we knew we would see her again. It was an amazing moment.

Amy is a naturally effervescent person and always has been. Being gregarious, she was always chosen for the fun roles in plays and, well, often got in trouble for that same thing while in school! But the trauma of being carjacked, realizing you've been shot, and then waking up to hear what happened during surgery took a lot of that away. Her room was dark and as cold as a Canadian winter due to medications, making her feel constantly hot, and the atmosphere was just quiet. It was so unlike Amy. There was occasional joking around, but it was just different, hard to explain.

About the time Amy was moved to a step-down unit, Adam received a call for us to meet with the city of Hoover's police chief because officers had captured the people who shot Amy. Even that was surreal as we all rushed to the police station and were introduced to various detectives who were on her case—because there were three police departments working on it! Why? Because she was abducted in Homewood, shot in Hoover, and had her car abandoned in Vestavia—all in the small corner where all those communities meet. The police chief seemed like the quintessential TV crime show officer—impeccably dressed, firm, and forceful and not above a bit of colorful language! He answered almost all our questions as best as he could without saying anything to hurt the legal case. We left feeling a bit of euphoria because the thugs had been caught so quickly.

After that meeting, I headed back home to Decatur to get more clothes to wear, work on the house, cancel mail, etc. Upon returning, Amy's room was still dark, cold, and quiet. She was hurting both physically and mentally. She has related the story about her physical therapist and her nurses, who so impressed me. Most of those young ladies were around Amy's age, and I felt they sympathized for her in a way that just seemed different, perhaps because of her age. Dr. George once said, they knew Amy was a true crime/gunshot victim as they get a lot of them. When asked why, he said, "She was clean—nails done, just clean". Amy also joked with her surgeons before going under, creating a relationship that lasted after she was released. Between sessions of getting her vitals taken, drainage tubes checked, and wounds packed and unpacked, there was a lot of silence and quietness. Sometimes, that quietness was broken by screams of pain from a nearby room. Being there was unsettling many, many times.

I recall one day, maybe two weeks in, after Amy got the disappointing news that she wouldn't get to go home the next day, my parents and aunt Carolyn came to visit. Amy just stared straight ahead. It was unnerving. When you asked her a direct question, she turned to talk to whomever but then resumed her silence and staring into space. It was truly heartbreaking as, well, what do you say? What do you do? Daddy had stepped out with Adam, and Mother was trying not to cry because it was just so unlike Amy. After a short time, she just said it was time to go, and when she said goodbye to Amy, Amy responded—and that was about it. Mother said she just cried and cried after they left, and I can see why. It is so hard to explain—that silence when you don't know what's going on in her head and feeling useless in wanting to help but not knowing how.

Sometimes, I got phone calls and messages from people I hadn't heard from in ages. A college friend, Anita McCaghren Smith, called to the room, which was surprising because *no* one was getting through to her room because the media was being so pushy. Her husband is a pastor, so perhaps that was why, or as I prefer to think, God *knew* I needed to hear from someone! While I did get those calls, I did not get very many from my church family at that time or from those I felt would. That silence added to the silent coldness of some of those days. I would drive back to Granny's house to stay with her at night and, at times, feel consumed with self-pity and loneliness that I heard from no one. Later, most of those same people all said, "I didn't want to bother you." Now I am a proponent of calling, texting, emailing, or sending a card to people who are hurting, whether it be from an accident, sickness, or other maladies of life. They need your message, even if it's just a short "Thinking and praying for you right now. You don't have to reply. I just wanted you to know." From a woman who has never been accused of being thrifty with her words, trust me, a short message is all someone needs to feel loved, thought of, and cared for.

After a while, Amy's room seemed to brighten a good bit. Her walls were being covered with all sorts of get-well cards, both bought and handmade. The handmade ones were probably the most enjoyable as they would come in a Manila envelope sent by someone's Sunday school class, who had prayed for her. Some didn't even know her but had heard about her from the news or a friend of a friend. The room was still quieter than the normal Amy, but it seemed that, perhaps, we were on our way.

Once she was finally dismissed, Adam, his family, and I came up with a plan to stay with her. Her nieces, family, and friends decorated their house for her homecoming. We had a quiet but nice evening of just being home after about a month or so of hospital stuff. Every day, I came from Adamsville to stay with Amy during the day and went back to Adamsville to stay with Granny at night. Amy had lost so much weight while in the hospital that she really looked more like she had, had a bout with cancer. So it was this mama's job to fatten her up by making her favorites every day. But the anxiety and stress from the whole thing kept her from eating much. That was definitely understandable.

About ten days or so after her second release, she wanted to go to the Galleria mall after one of her weekly doctor's appointments to use a gift card someone had given her to "go have a little fun." We decided to get a wheelchair in case she couldn't walk that far (and she couldn't), which led to a funny but awkward moment with a food court guy next to our destination store. He looked at Amy, who I guess just looked perfectly normal to him, and said, "What are *you* doing in that wheelchair?" He had a smile on his face that quickly faded after she said, "I was carjacked and shot!"

He stammered, started apologizing left and right for being so insensitive, and then gave us a meal ticket on him! After we got her shopping done, we were headed out of the mall, walking ever so slowly. It was obvious to others she wasn't well, as you could also see her drain. An older Black man stopped to hold the door open for her—and as we got closer, she had a vice grip on my arm. As I thanked him and he responded with polite, kind words, Amy was trembling and trying not to cry. Then she did cry because she was *mad*—*mad* at her reaction to a kind Black man, who just wanted to help, *mad* at her attacker for causing her to fear! Her response was to his race because her attacker was also Black. We have always tried to not think a thing about the color of someone's skin, and here, in an innocent moment, the ugliness of such fear was there. Would this continue to be a thing? She did *not* want to fear random people by association, just because they were Black. I wasn't able to say a lot, except that I felt that such fear would fade over time and that it was normal. What if the perpetrator had a big nose and curly, blonde hair? The fear might only return when someone really looked like her attacker, not just any random Black person. This incident has always stuck with me. Fear triggered by similarities is strong. I know of a woman who avoids all tunnels because she was once kidnapped and led to a building that was tunnellike. Her fear is very real.

Years later, when Amy and I were talking about the incident, she did not recall it at all! It was such a stark moment for me yet not for her. That fear had been removed—so much so that even a seemingly memorable event was erased from her memory. God removed that fear because He knew that He had plans for her to one day be the mother of a biracial child. There are *no* mistakes in God's design for our lives. None. Considering no mistakes in God's plan for us, the day of Keundre's sentencing, parking was at a premium and I was the only one in the family who actually parked directly across the street from the federal courthouse. After the sentencing was over, we were standing outside, in true Southern style, deciding where we needed to go eat. Since I was parked closest, I volunteered to go on ahead and get enough tables since they were walking a good way. As I approached my car, an older black man gets out of the car in front of me and asks if he can speak to me. (Now, my mother says we were standing in the middle of the street—I don't recall that part! Haha!) I said yes as I thought he may be one of Keundre's family members. He was his grandfather and wanted to know first if Amy was going to be okay. I told him yes, that she was all healed from the ordeal. His shoulders lifted, and he said thank God. He had been praying for her since the day he found out that his grandson had shot her. He said he watched every newscast and read every article, wanting to keep up with her recovery. He went on to apologize for it all. He said Keundre's dad left early on, and that he himself had not been much better as a father and he felt he carried blame too. He was holding back tears as he talked about hitting his knees when he heard on the news that she had lost a kidney as a result of his grandson's actions— as he was on dialysis, but that was his doings and his fault. Amy was totally innocent. He prayed that her remaining kidney remain healthy all her life. He asked forgiveness for his failings, and by this time we are both crying. This man was totally broken and totally sincere. I told him that no matter what happened when he was younger,

Keundre still chose to do what he did. Even those with 'good' childhoods do bad things too. I told him it was also no mistake that out of all the cars parked here, that the two of us were parked next to each other. We hugged and parted ways. Needless to say, I was the last one to get to the restaurant, and I couldn't tell everyone right away as to what had transpired, as it was too emotional. Seeing his grandfather's reactions, his deep regret, and sorrow shows yet another side of such crimes. As the criminals families also become victims too, or at the very least, they suffer as well.

Amy willingly shares her story, as do all of us. It is a fascinating story of intrigue, the kind of stuff you see on TV crime shows, which took me a very long time to ever watch again because they were too close to home. The first time I heard her share her testimony was at her home church—the one she grew up in. It was a ladies' night, so many were there that she didn't know—but also many women who influenced her life in one way or another. As she was sharing her testimony, we were *laughing*. I was struck by that laughter—the stuff we didn't have in her hospital room every much. Fifteen months later, I was laughing at her, retelling parts of the most horrifying times in our lives, and once again, it was surreal.

In the years since then, I have shared her story with both Christians and non-Christians alike. The most memorable was with a craft show roommate, who was not a Christian, a lady who didn't like me to talk much because she wanted to tell her stories. I had prayed for God to give me an opportunity to somehow witness to her, but in ten days of living with a hard woman, who cussed like a sailor, drank like a fish, and had to have things her way—I just didn't think it was going to happen. On our last night together, she turned the TV to one of the crime documentaries, not bothering to ask but just saying, "You like this stuff, right?"

The show was about a young woman who was kidnapped and killed, and her parents were being interviewed. She said to me, "I don't know how a parent would react to getting such a phone call."

Ding, ding, ding! There was the opening that God provided for me! I just said, "Well, I can tell you!"

I started telling our story, and she was constantly interrupting me with questions. After not even five minutes, she said to me, "I'm too drunk to listen to the rest of this, so you have to tell me in the morning all that happened. All I want to know right now is, did they catch the bastards?"

I laughed and said yes, and she said, "Well, good," and went on to bed.

The next morning was Sunday. I normally go to the church service at the craft fair, but that Sunday, I was having church in the condo! As we were getting dressed, I started over with the story because she couldn't remember it all! She was quiet and seldom interrupted, except with an occasional "holy s———" or such as that. When I told her the part about the angels—she was astounded. She was so receptive that I felt bold enough to continue with the peace that passes all understanding and how only our faith in Christ— peace that only *He* can provide—got us through it all, that even if Amy would have died, we *still* had hope because we would one day see her again.

She asked me if I really believed all of that, and I told her I did. She had been raised Catholic but never really knew anything but that. (We had discussed such several days earlier, when she pronounced me to be churchy.) Time prohibited our talk from going further, and since it was the last day, I didn't see her any more after that day or since. I did overhear her telling her booth mate about it, although it was a much more colorful version. She has been prayed for since then, and I pray she has had others in her life that will bring her to a saving knowledge of our Lord.

That encounter was yet another affirmation that God uses even our worst hurts to further His kingdom. It was literally the most casual witnessing of any kind that I've ever experienced— brushing my teeth, fixing my hair and makeup, all while letting Amy's story pour out. God uses our pain to help and encourage others. Our experiences and trials are jumping off points to share about *Him*. We don't have to have four points and a poem or have just the right scriptures memorized to get across that Jesus loves them and died for them and that accepting Him changes your life now and forever.

You intended to harm me, but God intended
it all for good…(Genesis 50:20 NLT)

We *all* have our stories, some plain and simple, others not so simple. People want to know our stories. They do not have to be dramatic but just tell what Jesus has done for us. For each of us, that *is* our own story, which makes sharing about Jesus so much easier. We are the ones who have lived it. We just have to share it.

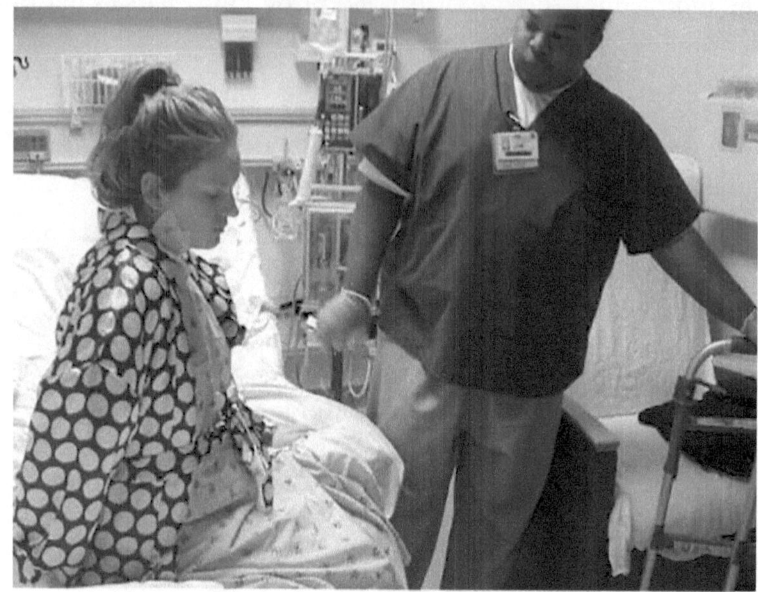

My first time trying to walk in the hospital.

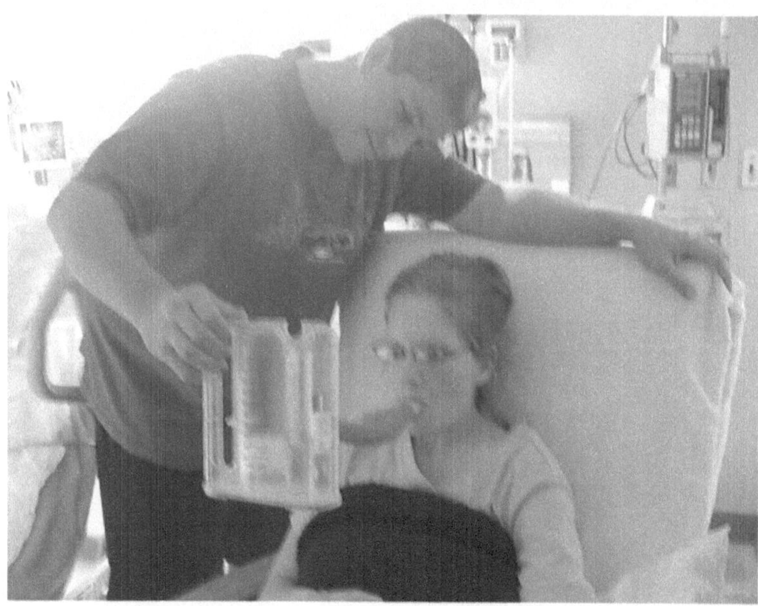

Adam helping me with my breathing exercises.

One wall in my room adorned by cards and drawings from friends, family, and people that just heard about my shooting.

Our homecoming after the hospital stay

Woman shot during carjacking; two in custody

August 2, 2006 at 4:07 PM CDT - Updated July 3 at 1:02 PM

Authorities say two people are in police custody in connection with at least three carjackings.

One of the carjackings involved Decatur native Amy Holaway Rogers.

A U.S. Marshal says an 18-year-old man and a 28-year-old woman were arrested last night and taken to the Hoover police department.

In Monday's carjacking, Rogers was abducted at

Part of news article from my accident

About the Author

Amy Rogers was born and raised in the beautiful state of Alabama. She considers her faith, family, and friends to be most important to her. She loves being the only woman in the house with her husband and two boys. She pours into the lives of children daily as an educator. She enjoys traveling to see different parts of our world. She's also a little obsessed with gnomes. She loves to make people laugh.

In her first book, you may laugh and cry, along with her, as she opens up about the trials in her life and how God brought her out victorious.